MW00878926

# Into the Heart of Health

### REACHING YOUR HEALTH THRESHOLD, AN UNSHAKEABLE BALANCE IN MIND, BODY, AND EMOTIONS

## DR. EVELYNE LEONE

**BALBOA.**PRESS
A DIVISION OF HAY HOUSE

Copyright © 2021 Dr. Evelyne Leone.

All rights reserved. No part of this book may be used or reproduced by
any means, graphic, electronic, or mechanical, including photocopying,
recording, taping or by any information storage retrieval system
without the written permission of the author except in the case of
brief quotations embodied in critical articles and reviews.

Balboa Press books may be ordered through booksellers or by contacting:

Balboa Press
A Division of Hay House
1663 Liberty Drive
Bloomington, IN 47403
www.balboapress.com
844-682-1282

Because of the dynamic nature of the Internet, any web addresses or
links contained in this book may have changed since publication and
may no longer be valid. The views expressed in this work are solely those
of the author and do not necessarily reflect the views of the publisher,
and the publisher hereby disclaims any responsibility for them.

The author of this book does not dispense medical advice or prescribe the use
of any technique as a form of treatment for physical, emotional, or medical
problems without the advice of a physician, either directly or indirectly. The
intent of the author is only to offer information of a general nature to help
you in your quest for emotional and spiritual well-being. In the event you use
any of the information in this book for yourself, which is your constitutional
right, the author and the publisher assume no responsibility for your actions.

Any people depicted in stock imagery provided by Getty Images are
models, and such images are being used for illustrative purposes only.
Certain stock imagery © Getty Images.

Print information available on the last page.

ISBN: 978-1-9822-6141-2 (sc)
ISBN: 978-1-9822-6143-6 (hc)
ISBN: 978-1-9822-6142-9 (e)

Library of Congress Control Number: 2021900329

Balboa Press rev. date: 02/05/2021

To my children, whose wisdom mesmerizes me more every day. They have showed me the power of love.

To my parents, who both miraculously survived World War II and taught me strength and resilience and how to never take life for granted.

To my two uncles, both named Gilbert, who knew that cultivating and spreading joy was not only essential for human relationships but also an ultimate source of success. "From joy comes forth all creation," and they lived up to the calls of their boundless hearts to build businesses that have left a long legacy. I have been extremely blessed to grow up witnessing their energy in motion, even in the most challenging times of their careers. It has taught me how to keep my heart at peace during the struggles.

To my psychology mentor, Dr. Alemany, who supported my decision to enter medical school at the age of forty-four.

To Louise Hay, who has changed my life and the lives of many through her words. She inspired me to accept and explore the healing power of self-love and trust our intuition in the mind-body connection. Her presence in this world is forever shining.

To my mentor and dear friend Dr. Jean Houston, who helped me see far beyond the limitations of my mind to reach my highest potential.

To my spiritual teachers, Dr. Dao Le and Dr. Joseph Michael Levry, whose unconditional love has guided me and is still supporting me into the healing journey of life.

To my physician colleagues who, like me, are pioneers of a new paradigm, bringing consciousness to the field of medicine.

To my dear friends and family members in Florida, California, Oregon, Texas, New Jersey, Mexico, France, and Sweden who have supported me with unconditional love during a new life journey into the unknown, both in my career and personal life.

To the Naam Yoga community, who is continuously blessing me and my children with love, peace, and light.

"Dr. Leone takes us to the very root of today's most prevalent health challenges so they may be unraveled at the level of the source. Into the Heart of Health is a brilliant book that presents the ultimate foundation for bringing about permanent cures, reversing the aging process, overcoming physical, mental or emotional challenges and much more. In this rapidly changing and unpredictable world, Dr. Leone stands boldly and beautifully among those health professionals who are both willing and equipped to deliver the facts about the true nature of healing, that no human being should be without."

-DR. JOSEPH MICHAEL LEVRY, CEO of Rootlight, Author, Composer, and World-renowned Spiritual Leader.

"I have known Dr. Leone for years and I find her to be a remarkable combination of being at the very forefront of modern medicine, a pioneer in understanding our psychological depths, a master of spiritual healing, and a leading-edge thinker in the emerging field of functional medicine. In her concept and practice of the Health Threshold, Dr. Leone shows us how mental toxins sabotage our life force and how to find the frequency wave - the profound pattern of the body's music - that clears it of illness and sends ageism into obsolescence."

-JEAN HOUSTON, PH.D., Chancellor of Meridian University, Author of The Possible Human, The Wizard of Us, and many, many more.

"Dr. Leone's book helps you restore your health, causing your fears to vanish and catalyzing your inner healing! Her poetic and eloquent heart expresses itself with clarity and inspiration that sees love, joy, and resilience as the means to overcome adversity. She wisely recognizes love as the fuel of all creation encouraging others to appreciate what is already within them."

- JORGE FRANCIS CASSIR, MD, Author, CHP Coach

"I cannot say enough about Evelyne, who has been on an advanced journey in health and now has shared her deep wisdom in Into the Heart of Health'. This book ignites me to pursue a greater level of well-being through her brilliant tools and exercises that integrate the mind, the body, and the spirit. This is a **must-read** for everyone! It takes to heart the methods and tools that lie at the seat of our well-being, anti-aging, and disease-free life! Congratulations to Evelyne, and all who read this book!"

- SANGEETA PATI, MD, FACOG, Renowned Restorative Medicine Practitioner, founder of Sajune Institute for Restorative and Regenerative Medicine

"Dr. Evelyne Leone has the unique combination of traditional medical training paired with a holistic approach. She incorporates this approach with a total focus on the body, mind, senses, and spirit. She sees each person in their entirety and focuses on the perfect combination to meet each individual's unique needs. As a psychologist, I appreciate this distinctive approach because it has helped my patients achieve total health. Her book, Into the Heart of Health, is an excellent guide to all her techniques to achieve good health and emotional balance."

- LANA M. STERN, PH.D., Licensed Psychologist, Founder of Florida Collaborative Trainers

"Dr. Leone stays abreast of all the latest research in longevity medicine. I can count on her to be informed of the pros and the cons of the latest therapies available. Her warmth and her compassionate nature balanced with this scientific mind are the perfect combinations for a physician in this day and age."

- CARYNA FERNANDEZ, Certified Hypnotherapist

"Dr. Evelyne Leone joins her medical knowledge with nutrition, a great understanding of environmental factors affecting aging, and a treatment plan individualized to every patient."

-NYDIA QUIROGA, MD

# Contents

Foreword ........................................................... xv
An Invitation to My Readers .......................... xvii
Introduction ................................................... xix

*Chapter 1*
**Don't Take Fear for an Answer** .......................1

*Chapter 2*
**The Health Threshold** ...................................5
  · The Story of Dr. Andrew Taylor Still
  · The Inner Pharmacy
  · Melanie's Story
  · How a Diagnosis Can Affect Our Health

*Chapter 3*
**Your Body is a Miracle Factory** ...................15
  · The Fantastic Voyage
  · Our Inner Universe
  · Cellular Regeneration

*Chapter 4*
**The Gift of the Mind** ..................................21
  · Spontaneous Remission
  · Choosing Our Thoughts to Generate Good Health

- Rescuing the Mind
- Meditating on Your Thoughts
- Good Stress / Bad Stress
- Psychosomatic Disorders

## Chapter 5

## The Stress Cascade—The AHPA Axis

The Stress Cascade—The AHPA Axis.........................33
- The Effects of Cortisol
- Stress and the GI (Gastrointestinal) Tract
- AHPA Axis

## Chapter 6

## The New Paradigm in Health Care

The New Paradigm in Health Care.........................41

## Chapter 7

## What is Functional Medicine?

What is Functional Medicine?.........................47
- Your Health is Your Wealth
- Protocols
- Finding the Cause of Disease
- Disease Prevention
- Nutrition
- Exercise
- Sleep
- Replacing Hormones
- Medications
- Aging
- Epigenetics
- Energy

*Chapter 8*

## The Fear Trap ..................................................67

- Anxiety
- Trauma
- Panic Attacks

*Chapter 9*

## Depression versus Oppression ....................................75

- Physically Induced Depression

*Chapter 10*

## Understanding Addiction ..........................................81

- Alcohol and Drugs
- Pain Medications

*Chapter 11*

## Regaining Power over Your Health ...........................87

- Conscious Health
- Cellular Regeneration

*Chapter 12*

## Know Thyself ..................................................93

- The Respiratory System
- The Digestive System
- The Nervous System
- The Endocrine System
- The Immune System

*Chapter 13*

**Breathing for Your Health** ..............................103
- The Effects of Breathing on the Mind

*Chapter 14*

**Calming the Mind** ......................................109
- Meditation
- Proactive Surrendering
- Do Not React
- Don't Take Anything Personally
- The Word We Say Is the World We See

*Chapter 15*

**Love Your Health, and It Will Love You Back**............117
- An Extended Meaning of Self-Care

*Chapter 16*

**Natural Healing Tools**................................121
- The Healing Power of Nature / Plants and Animals
- The Healing Power of Music
- Finding Your Voice

*Chapter 17*

**Into the Heart of Health** .............................127
- Healing at the Speed of Light
- The Field of Energies
- Light Energy
- Emotional Health

Conclusion.................................................137
Appendix.................................................139
My Philosophy.........................................141
  · The Health Threshold
  · Imbalance is the underlying cause of illness
  · Preventing Illness is a Collaborative Task
  · Epigenetics: Health is something
    we both inherit and create
  · Imbalance in the body is often
    caused by an imbalance in the mind
  · The way we breathe can change our lives
  · Redefining Stress
  · Health Consciousness starts with knowing thyself

Practical Guide to the Health Threshold ...................155
Recommended Reading.............................................157

# Foreword

Did you know that you have the capacity for vibrant health? Did you know that your body can serve you in astonishing ways if you follow Dr. Leone's instructions to accept your body-mind as a miraculous factory for ensuring a new order of health and transformation? I have known Dr. Leone for years and I find her to be a remarkable combination of being in the very forefront of modern medicine, a pioneer in understanding our psychological depths, a master of spiritual healing and a leading-edge thinker in the emerging field of functional medicine.

Her tool kit and immense abilities are the finest I have ever seen. She is the healer's healer as well as being a wise and winsome friend. I myself, following her guidance, am taken to be half my chronological age and it gets very embarrassing when you go to your 60$^{th}$ college reunion and are taken to be your own granddaughter!

In her concept and practice of the Health Threshold, Dr. Leone shows us many things. Among others, how thoughts are things and how mental toxins sabotage our life force. She developed a series of Mind Guided Body Scans and guides us as to how we can call into being an inner Doctor who is uniquely aware of how the symphony of health and well-being can be orchestrated. Thus, in many ways this book is like a piece of fine music, with Dr. Leone being the conductor to a magnificent melody of true and lasting health. She shows you how to find the frequency wave - the profound pattern of the body's music – that clears it of illness and dissolves its symptoms.

For those interested in rejuvenation and slowing down the aging process, this is a consummation devoutly to be wished upon and an entrance into a quality of life both unexpected by ordinary medicine and glorious for the patient. It restores the innate wisdom to those who still have so much to give and must stay healthy enough to give it. For now, we find ourselves living in times in which our very nature is in transition. The scope of change is calling forth patterns and potentials in the human brain-mind system that as far as we know were never needed before. Dr. Leone offers us in her unique work the ways and means to send ageism into obsolescence and bring the mind of the sage into our time of need. Thus, what you will read here is the call to regenerative health not just of person but of society as well.

Jean Houston, Ph.D.
Chancellor of Meridian University
Author of The Possible Human, The Wizard of Us, and many, many more.

# An Invitation to My Readers

I am welcoming you to a new perspective on medicine and wellness. Intuitively, you already know how to create health in your own body and mind. You may not have experienced it yet, but you have the power to ignite your inner spark of health and happiness, and this is what this book is here to remind you.

Creating health is like cultivating a garden. As you keep watering and fertilizing its soil, it will feed you in return; it cannot be forgotten or neglected.

Start giving your physical and mental health the attention they deserve. When you "Love your health", it starts loving you back and you experience more energy, peace, and joy in your life. This state of well-being benefits you and all those around you.

I invite you to decide now, in this very moment, to never take your health for granted, and to embrace this new empowering journey into the heart of your health.

# Introduction

Health is a precious gift that we should never take for granted.

In today's world, where everything seems to be accelerating, we need to preserve our physical and mental health to respond to all the demands of a very fast-paced, evolving society.

Health has become a major preoccupation for most people, and the 2020 pandemic that came to shake the world reminded us that we have to pay even more attention to it.

Although we have the most advanced and sophisticated medical tools and pharmaceuticals to help us live longer, chronic, autoimmune, and mental diseases are escalating, affecting men and women of all ages.

How can we have hundreds of million people living with diabetes and depression worldwide when we have made so much progress in medicine?

The vast majority of illnesses are not random fate or genetics. They originate from specific causes that need to be identified to treat the actual disease rather than its symptoms.

After training as a medical doctor, I joined the growing field of functional medicine because I wanted to have more tools to target what was causing disease in the first place.

What I learned is that at the root of most illnesses, there is an imbalance. Whether it is a nutrient, an enzyme, a hormone, or a neurotransmitter, we could treat many medical conditions by regenerating this balance. When the body or the mind deviates from this equilibrium, we cannot process toxins as well, and it causes a breakdown of our defenses that leaves us unprotected against toxins and microbes. It can also create a shift in body chemistry responsible for all sorts of immune reactions.

For the longest time, medicine has been trying to put the fountain of health and youth into a single pill that would work for everyone. We now understand that health is a constellation of factors that cannot just be combined into a capsule or an injection. We can also see more clearly how the constant interaction between mind and body affects our health.

In addition, the one-fits-all protocol doesn't always work. We all come from a different combination set of genes, family history, and life experience, and we each have a unique human body, mind, and spirit. We are evolving every microsecond in our uniqueness, and we are constantly changing. So, since we are not the same as we were a second ago, the treatment we may have previously responded to may not work anymore.

Over the years, I have helped patients by replacing missing nutrients and hormones. Their aches and pains would go away, they would feel energized and sleep better, and their overall health would improve.

However, when they were under too much stress and becoming anxious, it could offset this balance overnight. They wouldn't absorb and benefit from the supplements as well, their energy levels would decrease, and their immunity would weaken. I understood that it wasn't a myth; stress could indeed kill us because it dramatically disrupts the equilibrium of the body.

We keep being reminded that most illnesses are generated from stress and told to stay away from it, but stress is omnipresent and inevitable. The stressors we encounter in our environment, however, are not the real issue; it's how we process them that matters. Stress is most harmful when we perceive it in a way that creates fear. When it is not associated with fear, stress can actually be a positive stimulating force.

Our state of mind has a very powerful impact on our health, and some thoughts can initiate and fuel disease. The power and complexity of our brain is such that something as abstract as a thought can materialize into a chemical reaction in the brain.

I finally understood how this mind-body connection was operating when I studied the biochemistry of the stress cascade.

This interaction between mind and body has been my focus as a medical doctor, as I have seen the power of *mental toxins* to cause illness. Often, the reason why we get sick originates in our mind, and we need to address this as efficiently as we would a physical issue.

My goal has always been to help my patients access vibrant health, meaning that they would feel symptom-free and energized and be more resilient to illness.

I wanted to help them rise to a new level of health, a threshold, where they could resist the attacks of stress. The *health threshold* is a new concept of health, introduced in this book, which reflects the state of balance we need to generate optimal and protective health.

At the health threshold, all the systems in our body come to their optimal equilibrium, and our ability to detoxify and resist illness increases tremendously, as is our ability to fight existing disease. As a result, the cells in our body are regenerated, and the aging process slows down.

How do we reach this threshold? By going into the heart of health to build an unshakable balance in body, mind, and emotions.

This book describes the steps to lasting, vibrant health. It will take you into the discovery of what a miraculous factory your body is and what a fantastic tool your mind is. Knowledge is power, and nothing is more important than knowing thyself. Therefore, I have extracted the content I gathered from many years of studies in conventional and holistic fields that will serve you best in achieving your health goals.

I first studied psychology and then decided to go to medical school to become a doctor later in life while I was raising my children. Although learning the science of the body through anatomy, biology and chemistry took a large prevalence over the study of the mind during my training, I soon realized that body and mind were inseparable and needed to be addressed together in health matters.

I also highly value the many forms of yoga and spiritual teachings I explored throughout my life, especially the insightful practice of meditation and very powerful ancient breathing techniques.

I believe in the power of combining modern medicine, psychology, and spiritual healing.

We would be entirely foolish to dismiss a century of unbelievable progress in medicine and consider only holistic approaches. However, it would be even more foolish to deny the power of the mind and the spirit over health. I embrace both perspectives and want to help bring a much-needed balance between conventional and holistic medicine.

I always wanted to prescribe meditation, the safest way to empty and calm the mind and overcome stress, because I knew it was a valuable tool to maintain the health threshold. Although it takes years of training for a yogi to be able to sit still amid chaos, educating the mind not to react in ways that affect our health is a very achievable goal. Still, many patients feel that it would be difficult to sit still and let go of the many thoughts on their minds.

How to integrate it in a medical plan became evident when I started learning powerful breathwork techniques derived from a very ancient form of yoga, called Sukshma Vyayama, that gave almost instant results. Health and happiness are only a mind shift away sometimes, and the best way to naturally control our minds is through our breathing.

I created a series of online programs, called Breathing for Your Health, where I share this efficient breathwork that helps balance many functions in the body, restoring energy and sleep.

There was still a very important part of what I was doing to support my own health that I had not included yet in my treatment plans.

What I wanted to convey to my patients was based on personal experience, not the objective scientific data doctors were using. I had discovered something that had helped me so much that I had to put it in a format that I could offer my patients.

Surely enough, I had to wait for the right time to come, when this idea could be received.

The events of 2020 came to highlight that we couldn't uniquely rely on modern medicine.

This set a new goal in people's lives, to build a strong

immune system—in other words, to be able to prevent illness.

For this, they need to step out of the box, and explore the tools that are not provided in traditional medicine, which I am about to offer in this book.

I developed a series of Mind-Guided Body Scans so you become the most important contributor to your health, becoming your inner doctor.

We all have within us an intuitive awareness about our health. We can sense when something is not quite right in our body. What if, instead of worrying about it until we have a doctor's appointment, we could find out more on our own and start the healing process?

What I learned in my profession is that when the inner and the outer doctor collaborate, patients heal much better and faster.

The Mind-Guided Body Scan is a mindful journey; you are first a witness to a process that takes place in your body. As you bring your focus inward, you get in touch with the origins of the sensations in your body and the thoughts in your mind. This is healing at the source, at the heart of health.

My intention is that this book will open for you the door to lasting health, longevity, and joy. You will find new tools to take care of your physical and mental health in quick and efficient ways. You will be able to maintain the strength, vibrancy, and uplifted mood that will keep you from reacting to stress. This is a new era of medicine where we are all working as a team to create the symphony of your health, and you are the conductor.

# My Story

When I went back to college and medical school while raising my children, it may have looked like I was having a middle-age crisis. I never spoke about the life-changing event that led me to pursue a medical career. I wanted to leave it in the past as if it never happened, unaware of how much I had learned from it.

It was in my early thirties and had recently given birth to my second child when I was found to have cervical cancer, a fast-growing tumor that needed to be treated aggressively.

This was a serious diagnosis, and nothing besides a routine exam could have indicated that I had such a disease growing in my body. At the same age, the famous actress Evita, wife of the former president of Argentina had lost her life to this insidious illness, and in many instances, this cancer was caught too late.

I was in such shock. I had survived a quite chaotic and difficult childhood, the ups and downs of running my own business, and my life was now threatened when I was just starting a family and needed to go back to work.

I went into surgery right away to extract the tumor and was hoping that it would stop the spread of the bad cells. My surgeon was satisfied with the procedure, but when I went to see the oncologist I was referred to, he found that the new biopsy results were showing more disease and urged me to undergo additional surgery, chemotherapy, and radiation. He said that although he couldn't promise that he would save my life, these were the only available treatments. The recovery from surgery was difficult because I had been anemic after my last pregnancy and I was feeling very weak. How was I going to find the strength to endure these treatments? I believed in medicine yet was questioning if this was truly the only alternative. Well, it seemed that the universe had an answer for me...

I was on my way to the children's section in the book store, lost in my anxious thoughts, wondering how I was going to survive this frightening situation when a daring book title strongly caught my attention *You Can Heal Your Life*.

At that time, I was interested in business and scientific literature, and would not have chosen such a book, but it was standing out to me as the only book on the shelf, and I just had to pick it up.

I started browsing through the pages and couldn't believe what I was reading. Louise Hay, the author, had written this book because she had, herself, overcome cervical cancer. She was describing how she had used alternative ways to heal herself, avoiding surgery and aggressive cancer treatments. She had an understanding of health that was coming from a very deep place of reflection, and her words were touching me so profoundly that I broke down into tears. I found such relief and peace in reading her story that I intuitively knew that this was the answer I needed and that I was going to be okay.

The next day, I called the oncologist's office, and despite all the warnings, signed against medical advice, refusing the treatments he had recommended.

I reacted out of fear and I would discourage anyone to walk out of a doctor's office the way I did. Declining treatment was a big unweighted risk based on an intuitive and emotional response, not on scientific facts. I was greatly inspired by this incredibly inspiring woman who could understand why she had been diagnosed with cancer and how to stop the progression. I followed her advice and changed my lifestyle completely, eating healthier, exercising, and especially controlling my stress levels and negative thoughts.

I went to see a new oncologist to have regular check-ups. I remember how anxious I was waiting for results after every visit, afraid to find out that I had done something foolish and could be in real trouble.

Time went on and after a couple of years, I was finally told that I was cancer-free. The "high-risk patient" alert followed me a few more years until it was not relevant anymore. Then I just put the event aside and went on with my life, never mentioning it to anyone although it had shaken me to the core and educated me in many ways.

In order to stop the disease, I first needed to understand the main reason why the malignant cells had started growing in my body.

We know about the overall benefits of having a healthy lifestyle to prevent illness. What we don't know as well is how the mind can affect our physical health. This information cannot be found on test results, but we are receiving feedback from our bodies and minds that something is out of balance and has the potential to hurt us. How much we pay attention to it can determine the course of our health.

It became so clear that I had been ignoring all the signals my body had been sending me from aches and pains caused by excessive stress.

I had to find a balance in my life that would stop these cells from further spreading. It was the initiating step into my quest for the Health Threshold.

I took my health into my hands and forever understood how precious it was. From this point on, I promised to listen to my body, care about the way I felt, and do all I could to shield myself from stress.

This happened twenty-three years ago, and it was the beginning of a long journey into conventional and holistic medicine. It was also the time when I started immersing myself in yoga and mind-body spiritual practices with the Dalai Lama, Dr. Jean Houston, Dr. Deepak Chopra, and Dr. Joseph Michael Levry.

I wanted so much to understand how we could prevent and heal by combining conventional and holistic medicine that I went back to school and became a doctor at the age of 47.

Ironically, the way I started my medical career was by leaving against medical advice. It could have been a fatal mistake, had I not been able to regenerate the state of unshakable balance of the health threshold.

"Everything you want is on
the other side of fear."

- Jack Canfield

# Chapter 1

# Don't Take Fear for an Answer

You have already heard over and over that stress can kill you, but if you are reading this book, you are looking for a way out of this threatening stress cycle.

As a medical doctor, I could talk extensively about the things that have the potential to affect our health and take our freedom and happiness away. What we first need to understand is that it is not stress itself that gets us sick; it is the fear that is associated with it. The overwhelming growing numbers of stress-induced illnesses we are seeing today are arising from a society where fear has become predominant.

Our attention is solicited as never before, and we feel the urge to respond to everything because we are afraid of ignoring something important. We are bombarded by social media and emails, news and information about everything that is going on everywhere in the world. Technology has allowed us to have access to almost everything, and this can be wonderful—or disheartening and frightening.

The virtual world functions at the speed of light, while our human capacity to mentally absorb and emotionally process all this information has not caught up yet.

We are still feeling confined by the limitations of time, space, and especially emotions. As a result, we have an overall sense of being constantly overwhelmed.

We are so afraid of running out of time or missing out on things that could be valuable to us that we can't sit still and relax. This new trend has even given birth to a new psychology diagnosis called FOMO, "fear of missing out." This is just another diagnosis among many that is directly related to anxiety. Whether it manifests in FOMO, OCD (obsessive-compulsive disorder), or eating disorders, anxiety is the reaction to fear that eventually gets us mentally and physically sick.

Interestingly, we react to fear through the same fight-or-flight response that prepared our ancestors to defy the attacks of wild beasts. It doesn't matter whether we are afraid of losing a job or dying of an illness; fear is fear. We can naturally bounce back from a sudden fright as if nothing happened, but we cannot live in fear for too long, or it will affect our physical and mental health.

On the other hand, when stress is not fueled by fear, it is a stimulating force that keeps us alive and helps us perform so we can achieve what we want. We are under stress the moment we come to this life when we leave the mother's womb, and childbirth should be the most stressful and traumatic event of our lives; instead, it forces us to take a deep breath and inhale a new life.

We tend to give stress a very negative connotation. It is the invisible toxin, the enemy that insidiously gets into our system to steal away our sleep and our energy, to create all sorts of aches and pains and even the most life-threatening diseases. In fact, we are alive because of the stress hormone called cortisol that our body produces every morning. We hear about cortisol triggering high blood pressure, high blood sugars, weight gain, and sleep disorders, but we don't talk about how it benefits us.

I spent a lot of time studying the mechanisms of stress in the mind and the body and essentially realized that we can learn how to use stress to our advantage rather than being victimized by it. Fear materializes from a thought in our mind into a physical reaction in the brain that affects every part of our body. When short-lived, we have an innate ability to process it in nonharmful ways. However, when fear remains in the mind, it turns into toxic stress that threatens our health.

There is a strong correlation between stress and the epidemic of chronic and autoimmune diseases that we see today, especially with some serious conditions such as cancer. The idea that fear was at the root of many illnesses had been present with me long before I became a doctor. I decided to embark on medical school later in life because I wanted to know everything about the reasons we get sick and why some people heal while others don't. More than anything, I had to find out how to prevent disease and stop the recurrences.

What became clear was that breaking out of the stress cycle and addressing underlying fears was crucial in preventing illness in the first place. I understood that health is a collaborative process between body, mind, and spirit, where medicine, psychology, and spirituality should be used in collaboration. Traditional medicine has some of the answers, and holistic medicine has the other part. I also discovered that even the bad form of stress associated with fear only becomes a threat to our physical and mental health when we are below the health threshold.

"Man should study and
use the drugs compounded
in his own body."

- Dr Andrew Taylor Still

# Chapter 2

# The Health Threshold

## The Story of Dr. Andrew Taylor Still

One of the main principles that guided my medical career is the idea that when we create a perfect balance, the body can heal and regenerate.

On the first day of medical school, we were introduced to the philosophy of the founder of our school, Dr. Andrew Taylor Still, a man whose insight was ahead of his time. He had suffered the devastating death of his three children to an outbreak of spinal meningitis in 1864 after losing his wife to the complications of childbirth. It was extremely difficult for him, as a doctor, to survive the harsh reality that he couldn't save his own family. For the remainder of his life, he dedicated himself to understanding the human body beyond traditional medicine and finding alternative remedies.

His search led him to the conclusion that the body contained what it needed to maintain health, which was an inner pharmacy of the highest intelligence that could help the body self- heal. Our role as physicians was to find the tools to allow and maximize this innate self-healing potential; then we could overcome disease and maintain health.

He also discovered that when our bones were misaligned,

5

even in the most subtle ways, it could affect the function of our organs because it was disturbing blood and energy flow. He highlighted the connection between anatomic deviations and body chemistry. Furthermore, he acknowledged that there is a magnetic field to the body that also contributes to our health and can be regulated.

These innovative ideas were highly criticized and opposed by traditional doctors, but after facing such tragedies in his personal life, Dr. Still was determined to follow through and develop his own drugless treatments.

He designed a series of osteopathic manipulations and became so successful in treating patients that he eventually created his own school of medicine. He opened his doors to women and men of all ages and ethnic and religious backgrounds, going against the discriminative medical school acceptance at that time.

I have been very inspired by the contribution of this resilient man with exceptional intuitive intelligence.

I was listening to his life story and guiding principles at the onset of becoming a doctor, realizing that what I had always believed was now being confirmed by science. I, too, believed that, rather than just prescribing drugs, which had side effects, we could teach patients how to reach their natural physiological balance.

Prior to entering medical school, I had heard several holistic healers say it, but many of these concepts were too esoteric for me and not supported by science yet. It was only when Louise Hay's book *You Can Heal Your Life* had a significant impact on my own health that I realized how much more there was to healing than what we knew from conventional medicine.

Both Dr. Still and Louise Hay were not saying that

we magically bounce back from illness; there is a science and logic to it, and objective findings that agree with my scientific mind.

It is clear to me now that Dr. A. T. Still was describing what I see as our *health threshold.*

I came up with the concept of a health threshold when I was trying to explain to my patients what true, lasting health feels like. I knew what to do to bring them back to health and protect them from illness with functional medicine, but I didn't want them to rely only on external tools. I wanted to offer them the understanding and the tools to have power over their health so they could feel even better and be more protected from illness.

The health threshold is an edge where we stand in a state of unshakable balance. When we reach this health threshold, we unlock the door to the free circulation of the energies of health. This is the heart of health where healing can occur—and sometimes spontaneously. It is as if we reach a frequency wave that clears the body from illness and dissolves its symptoms.

It took me years of integrating everything I had learned from conventional, holistic medicine, spiritual teachings, and my own experimental healing practices to finally be able to explain this intuitive understanding of health with words.

I have been looking for the tools that not only help us bounce back from illness but also accelerate regeneration so the body can remain in a healthy balance. Ultimately, regeneration slows down the aging process, not for the sole purpose of adding more years to our lives but for prolonging quality of life.

_Dr. Evelyne Leone_

## The Inner Pharmacy

When the time came for me to practice in the hospital, there was not much room for exploring self-healing and prevention of disease. We were trained to respond to emergencies, saving lives with medications and surgeries.

Unfortunately, many of the diseases we were seeing in the hospital could have been avoided by regulating the body. I knew that we could prevent many of the diseases that were handled with aggressive treatments. I wanted to help patients reach their health threshold, but first I had to better understand the science behind this healing balance. What was this "inner pharmacy" Andrew T. Still was referring to?

The inner pharmacy is made of the substances that regulate our body and generate the chemical reactions that make our physical life possible.

Hormones and neurotransmitters are constantly released in specific timing and rhythm to create a state of homeostasis (physiological balance). They work together to stimulate our organs and make them function efficiently to sustain life and health. However, when we have too much or too little of a hormone or a neurotransmitter, it can affect the whole function of the body.

In turn, those hormones and neurotransmitters need specific nutrients to activate their production and release in the bloodstream. This is why we take supplements, especially in a world where we eat a lot of processed foods and the soil is being depleted of vitamins and minerals. Most people take supplements because they have heard it's good for them and they feel better when they take them, but they don't know what it does to the body. For instance, when

8

you lack iodine or selenium, your body cannot produce enough thyroid hormone, and you may feel the effects of a slowed-down metabolism, which often manifest with fatigue, brain fog, and weight changes.

When hormones, nutrients, and neurotransmitters are working together in perfect harmony to support body and mind health, we feel more stamina, our brains work more efficiently, our emotions are more stable, and as a result, we feel more joyful. This is because life energy is flowing freely giving rise to high vitality.

## Melanie's Story

I was a patient before I became a doctor. I know how much stress a health issue can put on one's life and how vulnerable we feel when we are suddenly diagnosed with an illness. I also understand how frustrating it is when no one can figure out why you are not feeling good and what is going on with your health.

Patients come to my practice with a wide range of issues, from migraines, sleep disturbances, fatigue, digestive problems, and eczema to more severe chronic illnesses, such as cardiovascular or autoimmune diseases. They are looking for alternative treatments to surgery and strong medications, or they want to find out where their symptoms come from and why they are not subsiding. Sometimes they want to optimize their health to prevent cancer, heart attacks, and strokes in the future or just have a better quality of life, fewer aches and pains, and more vitality.

When I first saw Melanie, she was experiencing many symptoms that were keeping her from enjoying her life. She was only thirty-nine years old and was always tired, complaining of joint pain, digestive issues, mood swings, brain fog, sleep disturbances, weight gain, and recurrent headaches. There wasn't one day that she woke up feeling good. Yet, according to all the doctors she had seen, nothing was wrong with her health. As it often happens, she had been referred to a psychiatrist, who had put her on an antidepressant medication, which wasn't helping. The next step was to go on a higher dose or add another drug for her supposed depression. Fortunately, Melanie decided to get out of the medication cycle and take her health in her own hands. She had heard about functional medicine and was referred to me by one of her friends who I was treating.

She told me she was eating a healthy diet, taking daily supplements, and trying to keep up with exercise. There was no apparent reason for her to experience all these symptoms, and after struggling with them for three years, she was almost convinced that it was all in her head.

We reviewed all her medical tests together, and indeed, according to her basic lab results, she was in the normal range of a healthy individual.

Melanie was one of the many patients we see in functional medicine who are at a turning point in their lives. They have given up on many of the activities they enjoy due to pain or lack of energy and only feel worse. As their lives become more restricted, they start feeling depressed and as a result experience more symptoms.

In order to break this cycle, we had to understand how it all started. In Melanie's case, it was right after the birth of her second baby, when she had to go back to work right away. It was also a crucial time because she was thirty-six years old, right around the age when hormones start declining. Women tend to be affected by the drop in progesterone, which makes them more restless and anxious. She was one of those heroic moms who did it all with minimal sleep.

Many people function in a survival state, like Melanie was as a new mom, by working long hours with little sleep, rarely giving a chance to the body to regenerate. We need a balance between work and rest that is more difficult to achieve in today's world.

We can exhaust our physical resources because we don't cope with stress as well anymore, and it starts hurting us. First, the adrenal glands get depleted of cortisol, the main hormone that helps us sustain stress. Consequently, the thyroid function may decrease, and eventually all the other hormones. It also often causes inflammation in the digestive system, and nutrients are not absorbed as well, leading to nutritional deficiencies.

In short, the body is starved from essential substances; we feel tired and become more prone to sickness as our immune function goes down.

As expected, when we ran more extensive blood work, we found out that Melanie was deficient in some essential vitamins and that her cortisol and thyroid levels were low.

She was relieved to finally see the reasons why she had been feeling so bad. It was not all in her head, as she had been told.

Within a couple of weeks, after we started rebalancing her nutrients and hormones, she was already a different person. She had regained energy, was sleeping better, and her pains were gone. She was able to gradually let go of the antidepressant and find joy again in her daily life activities.

Melanie's case is a typical example of what happens with many of my patients. They are functioning below their health threshold because they are lacking essential substances in their body, which, most often, is a consequence of too much stress. As they keep pushing through the fatigue, they end up burning out their physical resources. When this is not addressed in time and covered up by psychiatric medications, it can lead to more serious illness down the road.

## How a Diagnosis Can Affect Our Health

Melanie had almost accepted the diagnosis of depression and defined her new life around it. Doctors cannot underestimate the impact of a diagnosis on the mind of the person who receives it. Patients are already anxious when they come to see a doctor; our role is certainly not to fuel this anxiety even more.

Think about how much doctors have to be aware of their words when talking to their patients. From their place of expertise, they can either relieve the patient's anxiety or create more. When patients go home with a clear medical explanation and the hope that the illness will be well taken care of, they can attend their lives with a clear mind and be productive. However, there are cases where the doctor is in a hurry and just throws a concerning test result or a diagnosis at a patient and leaves without taking the time for much explanation and reassurance. I have experienced that myself and saw the effects of one word that made a whole week of waiting for their physician to get back to me a nightmare!

When we are alarmed by the doctor and not given enough hope that our condition will be healed, we can't help but worry about our health. Most patients start browsing the internet and identifying their symptoms with all sorts of severe diseases instead of doing their work or enjoying their families.

Sometimes patients stay away from the doctor's office because they are afraid of being diagnosed with an illness.

Medicine traditionally has a name for almost every abnormality, when sometimes it is just an imbalance that can be readjusted. A diagnosis is only a word, but it may change your life in a second, even when you don't feel very sick.

We now have names not only for illnesses but also for pre-illnesses. In an effort to prevent diabetes, we are screening patients for prediabetes. It is certainly beneficial to control blood sugars and keep them from escalating to high numbers, but why do we have to give it a threatening name? It becomes even more intimidating when we talk about precancer. Unlike for blood sugars, we don't know what can stop the shift to cancer. Patients feel like they are on the edge of a cliff, not knowing what could push them off of it. The stressful thought of the prediagnosis playing over and over in their minds can only make things worse.

This is disempowering and only results in more stress and anxiety, especially when you hear that the only thing you can do is take a pill that eventually will give you side effects!

We are more than a diagnosis or a number on a lab result. We are complex and miraculous factories.

"The greatest miracle on earth is the human body. It is stronger and wiser than you may realize and improving its ability to self-heal is within your control."

– Dr. Fabrizio Mancini

# Chapter 3

# Your Body is a Miracle Factory

We have a valuable reason why we should not let fear and stress rule our lives in the first place. We were gifted at birth with an incredibly well-programmed body and an infinitely powerful mind. Acknowledging who we are in body and mind should give us a great sense of humility and strength.

## The Fantastic Voyage

My fascination with the human body started when, as a young child, I watched a movie made in 1966 called *The Fantastic Voyage*. This captivating science fiction movie is about a team of medical researchers who are shrunk into a submarine and injected into the bloodstream of a man to save his life. As they have been made microscopic to the size of a blood cell, they travel through the blood vessels and become witnesses to the processes that take place in the body. They are transported into the cardiac vessels to dissolve a blood clot having to fight upstream against the giant power of the beating heart.

This is how I became aware, at a very young age, that there was a whole world living within us, made of things I couldn't see and sounds I couldn't hear. In this busy factory, a heart was constantly beating; blood was constantly circulating; oxygen was being picked up in the air and delivered to every part of the body. It was the magical symphony of life.

This traveling journey throughout the body captured me so much that I started going through the anatomy book I found on my mother's bookshelf. I was looking at the pictures and traveling mentally in my own body, visiting my organs going through the blood vessels. Needless to say, in my heart, I always wanted to become a doctor, and even though it happened much later than expected, I immensely enjoyed learning about this brilliant body we have been gifted with.

## Our Inner Universe

The body is a miracle factory that works relentlessly beyond our awareness, even when we are asleep, to keep us alive and to allow us to breathe, move, and think. Yet we go through the day taking this incredible body for granted and often only realize how precious health is when we get sick. Is there a more intelligent system than one that can orchestrate trillions of cells to work together to keep us alive?

The miracle of life takes place the minute we are conceived as this microscopic bundle of cells that unfolds gradually into an embryo. We start as a tiny dot, smaller than anything we can imagine, and become this human being who can see, feel, think, act, and transmit life on its own. It all happens through a fascinating genetic program that we have been trying to decipher since Watson and Crick discovered DNA. This supremely intelligent process makes each of us a unique human being, unlike any other.

We develop into a complete and complex human being as groups of cells gather and grow together. It starts with neutral cells called *stem cells*, whose purpose is not yet defined. Somehow they are naturally told to interact and transform themselves to give rise to different body parts and systems. Some are destined to form into arms, legs, eyes, and ears; some become our cardiac system, our digestive system, our nervous system, or our immune system. Every part of us is just a bundle of cells, and they receive signals from other substances in the blood that tell them what to do and where to go.

Ultimately, our bodies are composed of more than thirty-seven trillion cells that have come together to make our organs and serve many other functions, such as carrying nutrients and oxygen or producing energy. Our primary role is to feed these cells appropriately with all the foods and nutrients that were intentionally put on earth for our survival. When we don't supply them with what they need to keep functioning, we receive messages from our bodies in the form of symptoms, and most commonly, pain or fatigue.

## Cellular Regeneration

Nothing in the human body is static, and cells continuously die and are replaced by new ones. All the cells in our body come with an innate program, like a washing machine, that is completed in a specific predetermined amount of time. For instance, skin cells live three weeks on average, red blood cells about four months, and liver cells for about a year, while stomach cells live for only five days. As soon as cells die, they are normally replaced, unless something goes wrong in the programming. This is the regenerative process that keeps us alive and also changes us. We constantly evolve, and through the turnover of our cells, we are not the same person we were last year, last month, or even a few days ago. Every time cells die, we leave a piece of us behind.

It's estimated that the body, as a whole, regenerates itself every seven to ten years. The human body so far has been programmed to live about seventy-nine years on average, which means that we have at least ten major makeovers in our lifetime! Of course, we see many more people living beyond this average life expectancy, and this is increasing every day, giving us more chances to renew ourselves.

We used to think that this cellular regeneration didn't occur in the brain and nervous system. Our neurons, brain cells, were meant to last a lifetime, and if they died before, we would lose the function they served.

Although we still think that the regeneration of neurons is very limited, we have discovered other ways that the brain can change and evolve. This is what we call the *plasticity of the brain*.

We now believe that the mind has an impact on how cells come together and communicate in the brain, influencing some of its functions.

We already know that the mind has a direct effect on the brain. We all have noticed how we become forgetful or less productive when we are sad or anxious. The power of the mind goes way beyond this simple observation and plays a major part in the health threshold.

The mind is a center of
Divine Operation.

-Dr. Joseph Michael Levry

# Chapter 4

# The Gift of the Mind

Our minds are always in action; whether we are aware of it or not, our minds are constantly processing thoughts. The quality of our thoughts determines how we feel and has a huge impact on our health. As such, we can make it a gift or a curse.

We can have a very strong body, but when the mind lives in fear, it will eventually break down.

Doctors educate their patients about how to take better care of their bodies, but they also need to teach them how to nurture their minds. They first have to acknowledge that the mind is extremely powerful.

I believe that we can transcend many of our physical troubles through the great potential of our minds. My studies in psychology and my experience with meditation and spiritual teachings have given me essential complementary tools to help my patients. We all need to learn how to generate thoughts that protect our health rather than damage it.

## Spontaneous Remission

Something that especially triggered my interest as a medical student was what we call *spontaneous remission*. Between my rotations in hospice and intensive care units,

I witnessed some cases of what we would call miraculous healing.

How could doctors explore the human body for so many years and still not have an answer for the cases of cancer and illnesses that go away without treatment?

I started asking patients if they had done anything besides medical treatments that could lead to their recovery, and I heard the stories that other doctors had dismissed.

I remember a man in his late thirties who had been diagnosed with a large, cancerous tumor in his liver and had refused treatment. He came back to the hospital six months later, and to our surprise, his tumor was reduced to the size of a pea. He related the shrinking of the cancer to his weekly visits with an energy healer, describing unusual sensations in his abdominal area during the sessions.

This man had fearlessly denied medical treatment to trust a holistic source of healing in full hope that it would cure him.

There is a very interesting work from the Institute of Noetic Sciences that assembles the largest database and medically reported cases of spontaneous remission in the world. The extraordinary cases of patients healing from advanced cancer called my attention, as doctors reported that some form of positive thinking was involved, whether it was hope, faith, or just a strong desire to live. In contrast, when patients started to experience fear from the diagnosis, they would get sicker and wouldn't survive.

I believe that overcoming fear is behind the mystery of spontaneous remission. Fear puts a lock on our physiological processes, affecting our organ function and impeding the natural release of hormones and neurotransmitters. When we shift from fear to trust, relief from stress occurs spontaneously, and energy can flow again to heal and regenerate the body.

This is a more obvious application of what happens when we are regaining the fine-tuned balance where healing can take place, our health threshold.

## Choosing Our Thoughts to Generate Good Health

I always remind my patients that they have power over their health. One very important contributor is their state of mind, how they think and what they do with their thoughts.

Thoughts don't just randomly come to us. There is a whole history and experience that has given birth to every thought we have. When we become aware of this, we are more emotionally detached from our thoughts, and we can decide whether we want them or not. We become the conductors of our own life symphony.

Our minds are meant to be creative tools, not receptacles for emotions. When we let our emotions choose our thoughts, we are disempowered. We are at the risk of falling into stagnation and over analysis, which, as we will see later, can lead to depression. It stops our creativity and productivity, impedes our happiness, and eventually affects our health.

As the mind greatly influences the health of the body, we need to learn how to use it to our benefit. There is no worthwhile purpose in using such an amazing tool to make us feel bad and sick. Wouldn't you agree that we were not put on earth to live unproductive lives and destroy ourselves?

Our minds can be very stubborn, and it takes some

good tools to make them flexible and useful. Sometimes they can act against our happiness when they can see only one side of reality. They can be blinded and biased by narrow-minded, conditioned ways of thinking that keep us from seeing what could be better for us. Our minds do not always serve our best interests and can actually become our worst enemies if we let them.

I believe the more we become aware of something, the more power we have to change it.

Some thoughts are totally unproductive and are just here to distract us, scare us, or make us feel bad about ourselves. First and foremost, we need to acknowledge them for what they are, because not only do they waste our time, they are somehow toxic to our health.

## Rescuing the Mind

We need strong and flexible minds that are adaptable to change to shield ourselves from illness.

Life is unpredictable, and we are not in charge of everything that happens to us. As we saw in 2020, there are circumstances that are way beyond our control.

What we can do, however, is embrace our power over our thoughts. As we go through difficult situations, it is very important to stay aware that in the end, we are left with the consequences they might have had on our health. Some serious illnesses can arise after exposure to stress, and we need to protect ourselves even more while we are in the midst of the storm.

Maintaining a state of balance at the health threshold can prevent catastrophes. There is both a physical and a mental component to this balance. We will talk about ways to rebalance the body with functional medicine and holistic tools, but let's first look at ways to use our minds to shield ourselves.

We tend to think that controlling the thoughts and the emotions that they produce is very hard to achieve. It may be a strenuous process if we just work on the mind itself, and it often takes years of counseling, psychotherapy, and self-analysis.

When we have a good understanding of the mind–body connection, it becomes much easier. We mainly hear about how the mind can affect the body, how stress in the mind gets us sick, but what we do with our body affects our minds too!

Since the beginning of times, people of different tribes and cultures have been healing themselves through dancing, music, singing, and deep, rhythmic breathing. They knew how to use their bodies, the vibration of their voices, and their breath capacity to feel more empowered when faced with fear and oppression.

The ultimate outcome of these rituals was to free the mind. When we move our bodies and breather deeper, we activate the blood flow to all our organs. As a result, our brain cells are receiving more oxygen and our minds become clearer. It lifts up the "Brain fog" that makes us feel anxious. We become calmer and more joyful as clarity of mind brings peace to the heart.

As a human being, you have a feeling associated with almost every thought. This means that you already know how this thought is going to make you feel. Each thought/ feeling affects your body, and it happens instantaneously.

Choosing your thoughts doesn't mean controlling your mind. A thought arises with a feeling and triggers a reaction in the brain. When we attempt to stop or control the feeling, we create unhealthy mental responses that may help us survive but make our minds sick. The more attention we put into trying to control and suppress our thoughts, the more stress we add to it, making it stronger and harder to control. The thoughts and feelings we suppress will come to haunt us and cause harmful projections on other people. Rather than controlling, we have grown to learn that allowing is the successful route to mental balance. We allow the thought to arise and then decide whether or not we want to keep the thought.

## Meditating on Your Thoughts

Contemplating our thoughts without judgment is a meditative practice that calms the mind and makes us less reactive. At the beginning, it can be overwhelming because we realize how many thoughts we are entertaining at once. One thought gives rise to another, and each of them carries a feeling. We go around bombarded by thoughts and feelings we may not even know we have!

To add to the confusion, people we cross paths with have their own sets of thoughts and feelings in their own minds, and we project them on one another, creating more thoughts, more feelings. This is why just sitting in meditation can be torture for many people. We need to start with a practice that involves deep breathing, movement, and sound. It prepares the mind to be more centered by flushing away many of these thoughts. Then, when our minds are not as scattered anymore, we become fully present, getting in touch with our thoughts, which is very empowering. The mind cannot get stressed by the past or the future, and it becomes nonreactive. We don't become indifferent or insensitive, just more calm and ready to handle stress in a nonharmful way by selecting or changing our thoughts.

By having positive and productive thoughts, we can help prevent illness and even heal ourselves because it brings us closer to our health threshold.

As a physician, I had many opportunities to witness what the power of positive thinking can achieve. When it comes to health, our expectations have great influence on how our bodies react. If we expect a positive outcome when we are ill, our bodies will cooperate in the healing process by creating a supportive inner environment. The therapeutic effects of medical treatments will be enhanced, and medication will work faster and better.

Now let's look at the counterproductive aspect of life and what threatens the health threshold—stress and fear.

## Good Stress / Bad Stress

When I was training in the hospital, my daughter came up with a very innocent comment one day. "Mom, you always say that stress creates illness, but stress is invisible, so how can you treat it? So I know the cure. Since happiness is also invisible, it can make us healthy. We just have to replace stress with happiness!"

Indeed, I had to agree that stress and happiness are two opposite, invisible forces that greatly impact our health. My daughter was wondering why adults couldn't just choose to be happy rather than devasted by stress. It is such a simple choice in the mind of a child.

Children cannot conceive of how adults spend so much time weighing and analyzing things, because they don't.

It is not only because they don't have responsibilities and concerns. They quickly bounce back from tears to laughter because their hearts override their minds. In the same way, children bounce back from illness much faster than we do. I do believe that their innate positive attitude and their desire to be happy and go back to the playground is a strong stimulus that pushes them out of sickness.

What this conversation helped me realize is that we overuse our minds, often to our disadvantage, forgetting that our hearts have a powerful form of intelligence.

That leads to the topic of the interpretation of stress in our minds. It is not about stress itself; it is how we think of it that matters. Some tasks or events may sound very stressful to some people and not at all to others. This makes stress either a burden or productive tool.

There is a form of stress that serves you well, and it's called eustress (good stress). This is the stressful push we need to get started with a task or complete a task, the one that is energizing us in a healthy way because it is accompanied by positive thoughts. In this case, we are driven by the idea of a positive outcome or even the conscious decision of not failing. We are not oppressed by the fear to fail; we are positively activated and empowered by it.

When we are able to associate stress with thoughts of well-being, the stress cascade doesn't get activated, and although we are under stress, we are safe.

The bad stress is associated with negative emotions. It is caused by a sense of oppression or disempowerment in a situation, whether it is a work, relationship, self-image, or identity issue.

Often, it is the thought that we are not doing enough or are not capable enough, or that time is running too fast.

Sometimes, indeed, we embrace more than we can healthily respond to and are trapped in our to-do lists with a twenty-four-hour day that flies by. We may feel that life has piled things upon us, and we are fighting our way through to adequately attend to it all. As a result, we neglect our physical, mental, and emotional needs. We can intuitively sense that this might cause us to get sick, yet we feel like there is no way to stop it.

It becomes even more complicated when life presents us with challenging situations.

I often see patients who have had to unexpectedly change their lives to take care of a family member. Whether it is an elderly parent or a sick spouse, child, or sibling, they have to learn how to become caregivers. Their whole life suddenly revolves around their caregiving responsibilities, and they often have to cancel their vacations and stop socializing and exercising.

When I spent long nights in the intensive care unit, I witnessed many situations where people selflessly abandoned their lives to attend their dear ones. Caregivers become so immersed in their new role that they sacrifice their own needs, spending most of their time at the patient's bedside and interacting with health care professionals. They survive on a few hours of sleep and hospital food, and they are confined to a very stressful indoor environment.

How we think of stress is very important, and in many cases, we can change our perception of it to a more positive one that won't hurt us.

However, because of the nature of life, bad stress is almost unavoidable, and we also need to take all the measures to reduce its impact on our health.

## Psychosomatic Disorders

Psychosomatic symptoms are a perfect description of how a fearful thought can create symptoms and illness in the body. It happens as fear transforms into toxic stress in our body.

We all experience psychosomatic reactions, and most of the time, they are transient, and we don't put too much thought into the reasons they occurred in the first place. We don't need to analyze every thought that randomly gives us back pain or stomach upset, when the symptoms are gone. However, when pain and discomfort persist, it becomes crucial to see how these thoughts have now become a real threat to our health. As the psychosomatic reaction becomes chronic, it brings disorder, which translates as imbalance, and eventually, it may turn into a disease.

Psychosomatic disorders find their way through the stress cascade, which we have the power to stop to reverse disease in the body. This is self-healing at its source.

"It's not stress that kills us,
it's our reaction to it."

– Hans Selye

# Chapter 5

# The Stress Cascade—
# The AHPA Axis

Building stress resilience and a strong healthy body capable of surviving our modern environment and unexpected life events has been the focus of my practice. If the body can be brought to a place of balance and optimal physiology where it can defend itself, then we can avoid illness in general, even something as threatening as cancer. The stress cascade is detrimental to our health, our happiness, and even our ability to be productive. The health threshold is the antidote to the stress cascade.

When stress enters the body, a chain of reactions takes place, and the more it progresses, the harder it becomes to stop it. It causes a cascade of hormonal changes that can affect every organ in our body.

The very first thing that occurs is a thought or a group of thoughts trigger an emotion of fear. In turn, fear ignites the brain, and it initiates what is called the fight-or-flight response.

It usually happens so fast that we may not have the time to analyze the content and the meaning of the thought. We perceive a threat from our five senses; we may see, hear, smell, touch, or taste something that creates fear in our mind, and we react to it in order to protect ourselves. We may run away from it, or we may confront it. Either way, our whole being is on alert, and the brain is sending signals to the body to increase certain functions and shut down others. For instance, the blood flow travels to the arms and legs rather than the digestive system, as we are more likely to run away than sit for a meal when we are in a state of fight-or-flight. At the same time our heart rate increases, our eyes adjust to see farther by making the pupils larger. These are innate reflexes that prepare the body to defend itself.

As soon as we perceive a threat and sense fear, our nervous system is activated and causes a surge of adrenaline (also called epinephrine) in our body that gets us wired up and ready to respond to the situation.

At the same time, the amygdala, the part of the brain that processes emotions, sets off the alarm that alerts the master gland of the brain, the hypothalamus.

The hypothalamus then directs the stress cascade in the body. It starts by sending a signal to the pituitary to activate the release of cortisol in the adrenal glands.

This is what we call in functional medicine the HPA axis (hypothalamus to pituitary to adrenals).

This state of reaction to fear occurs to help us escape danger. It can keep us from getting hurt and be a lifesaver. However, like every protective mechanism, too much of it turns out to be damaging to us. The fight-or-flight response is meant to cause an instant reaction and therefore should be short-lived. No matter how strong we are, when we are repetitively or continuously hit by stress, we end up exhausting our ability to produce the stress hormone, cortisol.

In functional medicine terms, this translates to adrenal fatigue.

## The Effects of Cortisol

As we will see in the description of the endocrine system in chapter 12, we need cortisol to live. However, cortisol is meant to be released from our adrenal glands into the bloodstream in a specific pattern throughout the day.

When we are under stress, initially the cortisol levels are higher throughout the day, even at night, which often causes insomnia. Eventually, we wake up tired because we exhaust our reserves, and our cortisol levels go down too low.

The so-called adrenal fatigue is due not only to low cortisol levels, as we may believe. While cortisol is running high during the stress cascade, it depresses the function of the pituitary, a very important gland in the brain that orchestrates the release of many hormones.

The thyroid hormone is particularly sensitive to the effects of cortisol, and it often manifests in weight gain, brain fog, and fatigue. In turn, when the thyroid is not functioning well, levels of estrogen in women and testosterone in men drop, resulting in decreased stamina, depression, and mood swings. So when patients come in with those symptoms, we can usually trace them back to a period of high stress.

High cortisol can also have tremendous effects on our general health. It impairs the absorption of essential vitamins and lowers our immune system, making us more prone to illness. It also affects blood sugars and blood pressure, and long exposure to stress can lead to diabetes and an increased risk of cardiovascular disease. Too much cortisol can cause bone loss and lead to osteoporosis. It causes hormonal imbalances and can also dysregulate menstrual cycles and lead to infertility.

## Stress and the GI (Gastrointestinal) Tract

Our digestive system processes foods to selectively and safely extract the nutrients we need. They are released into the blood, which circulates to our stomach and intestines. Stress creates a reaction of muscle tension and superficial breathing that restricts the blood flow to the digestive organs.

Dr. Gundry, in his book *The Longevity Paradox*, describes how, under stress, the digestive system is deprived of blood flow, and it compromises the intestines.

The nutrients from foods are not of any use if they just remain circulating in the blood. The cells in our body have to pick up and absorb those vitamins, proteins, and minerals. We may have adequate levels of nutrients in our blood tests, but they can still be deficient in our cells, because under stress, they cannot be well absorbed and utilized appropriately.

The trillions of cells in our body need to be continuously fed with the right substances to keep us healthy. Stress gets in the way of this process and affects the cells by starving them.

Also, there is a link between our GI tract (our gut) and our mental health.

Interestingly, the neurotransmitter serotonin, which is essential for mental well-being, is produced in the gastrointestinal tract. Ironically, we produce less serotonin when we are under stress and need it the most!

We may prescribe SSRI (selective serotonin reuptake inhibitors) antidepressants to artificially produce more serotonin when depressive symptoms are persistent. It may be helpful, but the medication only covers the symptoms, and often, doses need to be increased. SSRI drugs have a wide range of side effects, and discontinuing them might be challenging.

We are learning more and more about the importance of taking care of our gut and all the bacteria that live there producing important vitamins and neurotransmitters. You may have heard that we are mainly made of bacteria, and that some are beneficial and some are harmful to our health.

Some of these good bacteria have very important roles, as they help produce neurotransmitters and absorb nutrients. So we need to have enough of them to do their work.

On the hand, other bacteria cannot be present in too high numbers or they may cause inflammation or infection. It is—again—a matter of balance, like everything else in the body.

Stress has a detrimental impact on the gut and causes a bacterial imbalance that can result in digestive disturbances, absorption issues, and mood disorders.

Stress causes what you may know as a leaky gut, which lets the beneficial bacteria escape the intestines and often results in having too much of the harmful bacteria called SIBO (small intestinal bacterial overgrowth).

The gut is a sensitive place for our emotions. Many people experience heartburn, for instance, and think it's all about the foods they eat. Yet there is, in most cases, a direct correlation with stress.

Energy healers often focus on healing the third chakra, which is located in the solar plexus around the stomach. This is considered an important center for our nervous system, which connects with the gut. When we experience fear, we can feel this area becoming tighter; sometimes we can sense butterflies. We can even have a direct reaction in the gut with stomach pain or loose stools. So, it is no surprise that relaxing this area is healing. Some of the tools we use to reach the health threshold create this relaxation as a baseline so that when stress arises, we don't have this unpleasant and possibly damaging gut reaction.

## AHPA Axis

I believe the HPA axis should be renamed the AHPA axis, adding A for amygdala. We cannot leave out the amygdala, because this is where it all starts. The amygdala is the part of the brain that senses the emotion of fear. Without this perception of the emotion, there is no fight-or-flight response and no stress cascade.

So, in order to eradicate stress at the source, we need to prevent the amygdala from sensing fear. In other words, transform the fear at its very source into a more positive, or at least less destructive, emotion. If we want to stop the damages of stress, we need to address it before it even enters our minds.

How do we do that?

By becoming very conscious of both our thoughts and our emotions as soon as they arise. This is a refined level of awareness that we can all reach when we start paying more loving attention to the miracle we are in body and mind.

The goal of my mind-guided body scans is to support you in this mindful and soulful journey.

"The person who takes medicine must recover twice, once from the disease, and once from the medicine."

– Sir William Osler

# Chapter 6

# The New Paradigm in Health Care

Now let's look at what is happening from the perspective of medicine and health care and why I chose to practice functional medicine.

Health care is facing a major crisis as we are confronted with chronic diseases like never before. Overall, we see more chronic conditions, both physical and mental, and we are still losing too many lives to the devastation of cancer.

Most of these illnesses are stress and toxin induced. Stress, as we have seen, is a major contributor, but the water and the foods that we ingest also hold a large responsibility for the surge of these illnesses.

We have become more aware of the problem of hidden sugars in foods, but many products still contain high-fructose corn syrup, which contributes to obesity and diabetes.

GMOs and other manipulated foods trigger autoimmune diseases, and pesticides cause cancer. Animals are injected with hormones and antibiotics, and so are their eggs and their milk. Our water is polluted with toxic substances, and it becomes more and more difficult to find its pure form. Our overexploited soil is not providing sufficient amounts of nutrients in our foods, and when we don't supplement our diets adequately, our bodies do not get what they need to stay healthy.

Medical doctors don't usually have the time or the training to address these environmental considerations. We have been primarily trained in saving lives and treating illnesses that are already causing severe symptoms or can be identified in conventional medical testing.

When patients struggle with milder issues, such as fatigue, pain, lack of sleep, brain fog, weight gain, gastrointestinal disturbances, or anxiety, it usually doesn't appear in a blood test. Yet those symptoms impair their quality of life and may be the first signs that a full-blown illness is developing.

Our health care system is not designed to prevent disease, and it is now being challenged by the cost of chronic diseases, trying to sustain insurance coverage and quality of care. As a result, people of all ages have suddenly become interested in wellness and engaged in their own health care. They want to understand how their bodies and minds work. This is creating collaborative relationships and interaction between patients, doctors, and holistic healers. Conventional medicine and holistic medicine cannot be separated anymore.

The vast majority of chronic diseases are not random fate or genetics. More people are diagnosed with diabetes, cardiovascular disease, and cancer without any genetic predisposition. These diseases originate from specific causes that doctors need to address in depth for healing to take place.

I chose to join the growing field of functional medicine because it provides additional tools to further identify what causes illness in the first place. When we unravel the origin of disease, getting to the heart of health, we have the elements to heal it at the source and prevent further occurrences.

Ten years ago, when I started my fellowship in antiaging functional medicine, not many knew about this new field of medicine, and it was not easy to be among the few physicians prescribing supplements and hormones to treat and prevent chronic illness. Over the years, the interest in alternative treatments has grown extensively everywhere as a result of patients inquiring about more holistic modalities.

Medicine is redefining itself, allowing patients to become more empowered with their health, and this new behavior promises major changes. In the past few years, we have reached what we have called a new paradigm in medicine. Patients have brought forth a new road to health care by becoming more informed through accessing multiple sources of shared knowledge online. What we are seeing is a patient revolution; they are asking for their right to be offered choices and their right to choose. Who wants to be given a diagnosis and told there is only one available treatment that may or may not work? There are multiple alternative options in holistic medicine that doctors are now more prone to consider in treating their patients.

In fact, this shift in medicine is not a totally new paradigm, because it is based on what has been practiced for thousands of years in different traditions and places. We are putting together the pieces of a gigantic puzzle to create one integrated medical world where all options can coexist, including Western medicine. We are bringing together the different healing modalities that have already been practiced, sometimes for thousands of years, in different traditions and places. We are now combining in a supplement bottle the experience of Chinese, Ayurvedic, shamanic, Tibetan, or Greek medicine. We import energizing superfoods from Asia, India, and Peru that cannot be found on our continent. Interestingly, all these forms of ancient medicine are aimed at regenerating balance. When pharmaceuticals were not around, healers knew that we could use our inner resources to maintain health.

Nowadays, we consult the internet for everything we need, and it is overwhelming how much medical information has become available online. Without medical knowledge, it's difficult to sort it out; sometimes patients scare themselves unnecessarily by browsing diagnoses, or they can be prompted to order a supplement that may be useful for some but harmful to others.

While browsing through all these symptoms and illnesses, they can sometimes develop what we call in medical school "the medical student syndrome," meaning they think they have every medical issue they read about!

People are spending time and money looking for online resources to find natural cures for their symptoms and protect their health. While a parallel market for alternative care is growing exponentially, patients are independently looking for guidance to preserve and optimize their health.

The problem is they don't know what is good for their specific needs. They buy the supplements recommended in an advertisement that pops up on their screen. Sometimes they try it because a friend swears by it, but just like with medications, we need to make sure we need it and it is good for us.

Medical care has to evolve into a true partnership where patients and doctors collaborate to make the best decisions. Physicians are stepping up to explore other forms of healing that could be less invasive and harmless to their patients. Not every illness can be treated as an emergency with pharmaceuticals and surgery. There are certainly instances where only conventional treatments work, and we need antibiotics to cure some infections and Epinephrine to stop life-threatening allergic reactions. However, wherever possible, we should use more natural, less invasive treatments that don't cause side effects.

Some medications can be very beneficial for short-term use to abort the symptoms, but eventually, we want to rebalance the body so it can fight for itself and become more resilient.

Some of my patients initially come in with medications that they have been taking for years. As we work on bringing them to their health threshold, they need lower doses of their medications. Many patients even gradually stop using them.

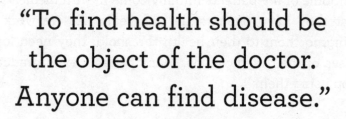

"To find health should be
the object of the doctor.
Anyone can find disease."

- Dr Andrew Taylor Still

## Chapter 7

# What is Functional Medicine?

## Your Health is Your Wealth

There is nothing more valuable than health, and we cannot take it for granted, especially today.

We need to be mentally and physically fit enough to withstand environmental changes and the stress load that society is putting on us to stay healthy.

Our world is evolving at a very fast pace with the incredible advances in internet technology and expanded worldwide communication.

We have to strengthen our general health and immune system to face pandemics as we are traveling the world and unknowingly spreading a microbe that can affect the health of many.

Fortunately, medicine is advancing too, providing additional tools to prevent disease and optimize health. Vitamins, minerals, and hormones are being further studied and tested for the purpose of building immunity. We are prescribing low carb, vitamin-rich diets that boost the immune system and protect the cardiovascular system.

Functional medicine is at the forefront of innovative testing and therapies to stop the disease before it manifests and the attacks of aging before they start. Functional medicine is a new branch of medicine that brings together conventional and holistic sciences to treat illness at its source and prevent disease. We use the least invasive and most natural treatments, avoiding strong medications that cause side effects.

It is sometimes referred to as antiaging medicine because it helps slow down the aging process. As we age, the body becomes more easily depleted of nutrients and hormones and cannot function optimally because it is lacking fuel. As a result, our cells lose their efficiency to process toxins or produce energy from foods, and we start feeling the negative effects of aging.

When we adequately replace those missing nutrients and hormones, we regenerate the cells, and they start functioning better. I often hear my patients say that they feel better than when they were younger, and they can sustain vigorous exercise routines.

In functional medicine, we look at the patient as a whole, rather than focusing on a specific part of the body, because disease can arise from a different place than the one it manifests in, even our minds.

We use personalized treatments that address each person as unique, taking into consideration their genetic makeup, lifestyle, family and personal medical and social history, and their state of mind.

For instance, what you eat, how often you exercise, your habits, and how much peace you have in your life are factors that are as important to me as your genes and the medications you are taking. All these are specific to you and, more particularly, the way you think and the life events that have shaped your mind over the years and continue to do so.

I think of functional medicine as "futuristic ancient

medicine." It is the blend of best of old traditional home remedies with the most advanced medical studies and testing tools.

I am forever thankful to my mother, who chased me around the house to give me my daily dose of fish oil and magnesium. How could she possibly be so convinced that it was so good for her children's health? I'm always amazed when I read studies showing significant results with the use of traditional home remedies. We all have some in our family ancestry, whether it kept being transferred through the generations or not. Somehow, my mother must have known that this would keep her vibrantly healthy in her eighties, despite skyrocketing family cholesterol levels!

The anti-inflammatory benefits of turmeric, which is naturally used in most Indian meals, is supported more every day. The powerful effects of ginseng, the grounding power of Ashwagandha, the calming power of chamomile and valerian—all these are undeniably good for us.

We are welcoming into the medical field the wisdom of plants that have been explored since the beginning of time. Before the era of pharmaceuticals, people had to do whatever they could, using what was available to them, to stay healthy. Back then, they could feel the regenerative and healing powers of sleep; they could find out which foods were most energizing or cleansing; they knew that the sun was good for them when they didn't know anything about its connection with vitamin D.

We are also bringing forth the pearls of ancient philosophies about healthy ways to conduct our lives. In the Ayurvedic philosophy, the connection to the natural elements is crucial, but the knowledge of oneself in mind and spirit is most important.

The mind-body connection works both ways; our body reacts to the mind and vice versa.

Therefore, we have to treat them both simultaneously.

## Protocols

As the opposite of a personalized medicine that addresses the mind-body connection, we have protocols.

Overgeneralization in treatment is detrimental to the health of some patients, and the same medical protocols cannot be applied to all. Treatment shouldn't be based on the illness itself but on the patient as a whole, and we have to take individual differences as guidelines. Protocols work well in an emergency setting, as we may have to treat patients aggressively to save their lives, but we have to offer more individualized treatments in the outpatient setting.

General protocols should be used in case of emergency and adjusted to the weight, age, and gender of the patient. For instance, many patients present with the same complaint of fatigue, and for this one symptom, we can find different answers, and each will be treated differently.

My role as a functional medicine doctor is to pinpoint what has offset the balance in their body and to address it efficiently. For instance, it may originate from a toxin, a vitamin deficiency, or a hormone imbalance, which we can detect when we run more specific in-depth testing. However, we have to be able to discern that it can also come from psychological issues, and these need to be examined and treated with equal attention.

## Finding the Cause of Disease

In traditional medicine, we use basic lab testing and imaging to diagnose patients. We first have to see an abnormality in a blood test or an x-ray. Once we have found it, we make a diagnosis and give patients the corresponding treatment in the form of either medication or surgery.

The problem is that when patients have mild symptoms that don't correspond to a test-proven diagnosis, doctors have no tools to help them. Very often, they are given medications that are too strong for their symptoms, and the side effects may create worse issues.

In functional medicine, we don't overtreat or undertreat; we aim to recreate a balance in the body. We look for deficiencies, imbalances, toxicities, metabolic abnormalities, or even genetic mutations that can contribute to the symptoms, but we don't rely only on medical testing to give all the answers. What is also different from conventional medicine is that we don't need a diagnosis to treat a patient; we can help the symptoms by optimizing the body chemistry with nutrients and hormones.

Sometimes the cause of disease is found not in the body but in the mind. The way conventional medicine is delivered in today's health care, there is no time to go into personal and psychosocial concerns. Most of the time patients who show mild signs of anxiety and depression are referred to a psychiatrist.

Old-time family doctors used to be closer to their patients and take those factors into consideration. They also had more time to talk with their patients, which was part of the healing process. By allowing more time for consultations, functional medicine is recreating the conditions of this old practice that is more nurturing to the patients.

## Disease Prevention

Although we are improving screening tools in conventional practice, many severe diseases that we see in the hospital could be better prevented. Hypertension, for instance, can kill us before we even know we have it. A vitamin deficiency such as B12 can cause neurological issues if it's not caught in time.

Prevention is addressing subtle symptoms and testing abnormalities before they cause a problem.

This is why the way functional medicine doctors read your labs is different. In conventional medicine, we use *basic labs* to determine whether you have a major issue, such as anemia, diabetes, or liver or kidney dysfunction.

When the numbers on your blood test results are not highlighted, it means that they fall within the range of normal. In other words, your life is not in immediate danger.

In functional medicine, we use *optimal ranges* for our lab interpretation because we want to catch trends that may endanger your life down the road. For instance, if your fasting blood sugars are above one hundred, you will be diagnosed with prediabetes by primary care standards. You will have to take medication to control blood sugars, or at least you will be told to exercise and go on a low-glycemic diet.

If your blood sugars are ninety-nine, this is considered a normal result, and you may receive a mild warning that you are getting close to one hundred. In functional medicine, we want to see fasting blood sugars below ninety, because it protects you from escalating into prediabetes and diabetes.

During the first consultation with my patients, we look at the lifestyle changes that would benefit them, especially with nutrition, exercise, and sleep. How we treat ourselves and our body determines how we live and how we age. Our lifestyle plays a very important role in maintaining the balance of the health threshold. We need to eat and exercise well, and we have so many options to choose from. We also need to respect natural rhythms, especially getting quality sleep.

## Nutrition

Food is medicine but ..

The quality of our foods is not what it used to be, as we have overexploited the soil in the past decades to produce more and to produce it faster. This makes it harder to obtain all the nutrients and vitamins we need in our meals. We still benefit from a plant-based diet with fibers and some vitamin content, especially when it is grown consciously and organically, but we need vitamins to complement our nutritional needs.

As far as diet goes, we have different tastes and preferences that we can't neglect for the sake of joining a new movement in vegan and keto diets or intermittent fasting.

Society has been focused on producing foods that satisfy our appetite and taste buds in the fastest and most efficient way. Fast foods were a response to a demand for instant gratification, leaving behind the healthy eating habits of our ancestors. How ironic that we are now advocating having a caveman keto diet to regain health! We have different dietary requirements due to our genetics, our blood types, our body types, our schedules, and our levels of activity. So we can't generalize and have a protocol that fits all. We have to know who we are and what we need to find the diet that will optimize both our weight and energy and, more importantly, make us happy.

Foods are part of the enjoyment of life, and there are many options available today that can accommodate our taste buds and keep us healthy. However, we may be eating the best organic vegan diet and taking the highest-grade supplements, and it may not make a difference. What good are nutrients if we don't absorb them?

Optimally, we want to convert each bite of food and each supplement we ingest into energy that our body can readily utilize. One of the main reasons we don't absorb those good nutrients is because we are in a state of stress. The foods we feed our minds and our hearts with are equally as important as what we put on our plate. Also, when our breathing is shallow because our mind is racing, our digestion is impaired. Taking the time to eat and appreciate our food is an act of love and self-nurturing. In this way, foods get processed efficiently, and nutrients are actually delivered to our cells rather than hanging out in the bloodstream and getting eliminated. Our digestive system, this fascinating factory that breaks down foods and extracts what is needed, functions best when we fully participate in the process with awareness. You can find specific diet recommendations in my Practical Guide to the Health Threshold and in my online nutrition program.

## Exercise

There is a form of exercise that is right for you!

As important as exercise is for our joints, our heart function, and our energy levels, it doesn't necessarily mean that lifting heavy weights at the gym or running marathons is for you. Not everyone has to become an athlete. All we need is to move our body. Although being an athlete fits the lifestyle of some people, others could go for a daily walk and get a workout that is sufficient for their unique physical requirements.

How much exercise we need is very individual and depends on our metabolism and state of health. Sometimes just changing a few habits, like going up the stairs instead of taking the elevator, can get our body to move more and help increase our metabolism. What is important is to initiate a change in our physical activity and get consciously involved with our body in a new practice. When we engage it with a happy mind-set and enjoyment, any form of exercise benefits us. Becoming healthier is an act of self-love, not a punishment.

We shouldn't do a form of exercise that we resent, doing it just for the sake of managing weight or keep our heart healthy. When our mind rebels, the benefits are lost because frustration will trigger stress, which in turn raises the stress hormone, cortisol. The results can actually be counterproductive, and we can exhaust ourselves on a treadmill, not losing a pound and not feeling healthier or happier!

Sometimes the healthy change is actually to exercise less or take on a more gentle form of physical activity. I see patients who are completely burnt out, energy depleted, and depressed after exercising intensively for months.

On the other hand, many people sign up at their local gym with the greatest intentions and give up after a month, or they postpone physical activity just because it feels like too much of an effort. When they feel bad about themselves for not following through, I remind them that we are all unique and we have different ways to reach our health threshold. Ultimately, it is that balance that matters most.

## Sleep

We say that food is medicine, but so is sleep. In ancient Greece, sleep was used as a medical treatment. The regenerative effects of sleep were recognized as very beneficial and healing to the body and the mind.

Did you know that there is a direct link between lack of sleep, or poor-quality sleep, and obesity and heart disease?

Just like nature has seasons, moon cycles, and tides, the body too has cycles and rhythms. Our natural sleep cycle can only be completed when we sleep long and deeply enough. There is a phase during sleep called rapid eye movement (REM), the dream phase, during which the body is very active. When we go through REM, our blood flow increases to wash off toxins, our brains accelerate to store memories, allowing the mind to have more clarity upon awakening, and we burn calories.

Currently, as much as a third of the adult American population is lacking adequate sleep, and we are seeing a new wave of teenage insomnia. Sometimes it's a matter of making enough time for sleep, but in most cases, people find it difficult to fall or to stay asleep. The result is that they are not getting enough REM sleep to allow their body to recycle, and it can lead to health issues. Sleeping aids may help temporarily, but they are not curative or preventive. Rather than having to rely on sleeping aids, we want to look for the cause of the sleep disturbance and address it at the physical, psychological, and spiritual levels.

While some people can still function with insufficient and disrupted sleep, they run into the risk of developing health issues down the road. It's often helpful to balance the body during the day with calming herbs and magnesium and use other natural sleep-supportive nutrients at night. Insomnia gives rise to a cycle of anxiety where the mind can't relax at bedtime, so addressing the issue throughout the day can prepare you for better sleep. Meditation and breathwork can also be helpful to restore sleep, as they induce the calming alpha brain waves. However, the lasting cure for sleeplessness is the balance of the health threshold. When we have hormonal and nutritional balance and feel calm, sleep cycles are naturally reestablished gradually.

## Replacing Hormones

In the natural course of aging, our hormone levels start lowering around the age of thirty-five, and as they do, the body functions progressively decline over the years. This makes us more vulnerable to illness and can affect our levels of energy, our weight, our memory, and our sleep.

Hormone replacement therapy is a major part of functional medicine treatments. We don't always prescribe hormone replacement, but we look at ways to reach hormonal balance.

Women were talked out of hormone therapy for years

after a large study made in the late 1990s, the Women's Health Initiative (WHI), showed an increase in cancer and blood clots. The women in this study were given high doses of oral estrogens that were not safe. Fortunately, the Menopause Society revisited this study and concluded that estrogen therapy given topically (through the skin) is safe and beneficial.

Rather than the high doses of synthetic hormones that were used in the study, we use minimal doses of topical bioidentical hormones, which are derived from natural products. Their chemical structure is also much more similar to the one that our body produces.

Both men and women can be affected by levels of hormones that are too low or too high and develop all sorts of symptoms, ranging from fatigue and weight gain to brain fog. There is more to hormones than sexual function and fertility; even our brain cells need estrogen (for women) and testosterone (for men) to function properly.

For example, many young women suffer from drops in or lack of progesterone. They suddenly become anxious, and they have trouble controlling their moods. They may have PMS (premenstrual syndrome) and are often put on the pill by their gynecologist, then sent to a psychiatrist to get antianxiety drugs. Sometimes they even end up on mood stabilizers.

Amazingly, as soon as we replace their progesterone hormone, they don't need any of these medications.

Other hormones play important roles in the body. DHEA (dehydroepiandrosterone) and cortisol support adrenal function for both men and women. DHEA was considered the fountain of youth for a few years in Europe, as it has an uplifting effect. They thought they had discovered the one hormone that would keep us young forever. It may be one of them, but we need others, as they function in harmony.

We also are very dependent on the thyroid hormone, the primary hormone that drives our metabolism. I see more and more patients with thyroid dysfunction, and commonly with Hashimoto hypothyroidism, which is an autoimmune disease. Whether it is related to toxins in the environment or stress is unclear, but it is very important to make sure the thyroid hormone is properly balanced.

Replacing hormones involves a clear understanding of everything that can cause fluctuations, deficiencies, and excess. It is a holistic specialty on its own.

We don't just replace hormones, especially not following a general protocol. We have to very carefully listen to the patient's complaints, look at the subtle signs of imbalance, and give only the minimal dose needed to rebalance health.

We also have to closely follow how the hormones are metabolized in the body and make sure they are eliminated properly.

Before we jump to hormone replacement, we have to think of all the other substances that help make and release hormones. For instance, the chemistry of hormone production is regulated by enzymes and nutrients. In functional medicine, we look at deficiencies or borderline low nutrient and enzyme values in the labs that may affect the production of hormones.

## Medications

We try as much as possible to avoid strong medications. However, I sometimes see patients who first need to be treated with pharmaceuticals or even surgery while they start more holistic treatments.

I don't encourage anyone to refuse or postpone treatments because of the fear of their side effects.

The biggest mistake is to completely dismiss conventional medicine and pharmaceuticals.

Certainly, things need to change in the way doctors prescribe pharmaceuticals. They all have side effects that can have negative consequences on our health when taken for a long time, but when we take a medication for a brief period to break through an acute issue, the body can clear it out without leaving any trace. Our digestive system and kidneys work day and night at processing whatever we ingest, detoxifying the body and eliminating what doesn't serve us. So I don't see a problem with prescribing medications if they are temporarily needed, as long as it is for a short time.

In fact, the use of a medication or even a surgery may be the very first step to accessing the health threshold in some cases. Sometimes patients suffer from acute symptoms that put the body in a state of chaos, and it loses its ability to regenerate balance.

## Aging

*How to Assess our Biological Age*

Our biological age is the one we should use to estimate how old we really are. Someone could be sixty years old (chronological age) but have the internal health of a forty-year-old person (biological age).

There are markers that are obtained in blood tests and

other screening exams that can show how fast we are aging. The main biomarkers of age are the telomeres, which are a piece of DNA present in each of the cells in your body. We recently discovered that the length of our telomeres is inversely proportional to our age; the longer our telomeres, the younger we are. Amazingly, studies have also shown that lifestyle, exercise, and relaxation techniques—such as meditation and breathing—have the most significant impact on telomeres.

Aging occurs as a progressive degeneration of our organs and tissues; it is caused by multiple factors, leading to oxidation and inflammation.

These cause chemical reactions in our cells, meaning that aging starts there, and we now understand that we can control this process to a certain degree. We can support and boost our cells to extend our lives and especially enhance the quality of our lives so that we can keep doing the things we enjoy. This is what we do in functional medicine, through lifestyle optimization and nutrient and hormone supplementation.

When we live a hectic life, we often don't take care of our bodies the way we should, and we may age faster without knowing it.

With foods being enhanced by preservatives, sprayed with pesticides, and altered by GMOs, our population is more prone to diabetes, cardiovascular diseases, and autoimmune diseases, which all contribute to premature aging. Switching to a mindful lifestyle helps decrease the risk for those diseases, helping us to detoxify from those harmful substances. We can also stabilize or reverse some of these conditions by gradually changing the way our cells operate.

Cells have a brain called a nucleus, where the DNA resides. The DNA is made of genes that send signals to activate the rest of the cell. These signals depend on what the cells receive, what we feed them with, and how much we boost them with supplementation, exercise, and breathing more oxygen.

## Epigenetics

We are not stuck with the genes we were born with.

"The human genome is a living text that continuously edits and rewrites itself," Dr. Levry has said.

Just as we can elongate our telomeres with meditation, we can also change the expression of our genes. This science is called epigenetics. Although your genetics determine many of your physical traits, it doesn't mean your genes should dictate how healthy you are and how long you will live. Except for some rare diseases, if your family genetics predispose you to certain health conditions, it is still only a risk factor, not a life sentence.

Many of us were born with inherited risk factors for cardiovascular disease, such as high cholesterol and blood sugar, or with genetic mutations that cause blood clots. Some of these mutations can result in conditions like cancer or Alzheimer's, but this is just a possibility in the big scheme of our genetic makeup. Yet we cannot just take a chance and hope for the best. We need to be proactive and do the right things for our health.

We have reached this new area in medicine where we can now obtain our genomic profile, so we can find out what we are made of and what to watch out for. Then we can use this information to focus on lifestyle changes and supplementation to keep those genes from creating illness.

## Energy

Before x-rays and blood tests, we used to assess health based on a more intuitive understanding of what was happening in the body. Ancient medical systems didn't have many testing tools, but they understood that energy was a key element of health. A failing heart lacks energy, a fatigued or depressed person lacks energy, and a slow brain lacks energy; without energy, we cannot live a full life.

Sometimes the body is not efficient at transforming food and nutrients into energy. In other cases, we may have a nutrient or hormonal imbalance, or we may be depressed and not getting the spontaneous push of the mind to get going.

Functional antiaging medicine also looked closely at the function of mitochondria, the little organelle in each of our cells where energy is produced through multiple chemical reactions.

In order for the body to produce energy, the mitochondria need to be fed the proper vitamins, enzymes, and amino acids. Lab testing can now provide a detailed report for all these; deficiencies can be addressed with supplements, and the function of mitochondria can be optimized. Along with hormone-replacement therapy, this is the first important step in this advanced way of looking at energy production.

Yet sometimes increasing the dose of nutrients, vitamins, or hormones will not guarantee increased energy levels, because the issue is in the mind. However, even mental issues can be treated as an imbalance, and with specific breathwork and meditative techniques, we can regenerate positive mental energy. Depression, as we will see later, is a state of stagnation, and we can actually reinitiate momentum in a stagnating mind, which will, in turn, regenerate physical energy.

Energy is a by-product of physical and mental health. Energy is not given as a birthright; it needs to be acquired, fed, nurtured, and preserved. If we stop eating, our body won't be able to produce energy; if we don't replenish our energy reserves by taking breaks and rest, our bodies will feel depleted.

As the medical intuitive Caroline Myss says, we have an energy bank, and we cannot waste our savings. We should plan on spending this energy intentionally and thoughtfully. Energy flows freely at the health threshold, and it manifests in vitality, unbounded physical energy, clarity of mind, and a sense of freedom and readiness for life.

Now let's look at some main issues that affect many people in today's society—anxiety, depression, and addictions.

"If you know how to handle
your thoughts and your
emotions, there will be
no such thing as anxiety,
stress, or tension for you."

– Sadhguru

# Chapter 8

# The Fear Trap

It's important to recognize the sources of fear within ourselves and in our society so we can address them efficiently. We are all subject to fear, but we are well equipped to overcome it. We also adapt to the changes in our personal lives and our environments because to do so is our human nature. Our minds are much more flexible than we tend to think, and our bodies can be extremely resilient. This doesn't mean of course that we wouldn't suffer from abusing drugs and alcohol and from the shortage of natural resources and pollution, but we are highly adaptive beings. We have an impressive ability to bounce back from illness and trauma.

We have been attacked and oppressed by real threats since the beginning of time when our caveman ancestors were at the mercy of being attacked by wild animals. Today, we may live in sheltered environments, but we have become hypervigilant and reactive, as if we still had to fight for survival in the same way. Our primal brain is being overactivated by the demands of the modern world, which adds to the burden of our existential fears of not having enough love, money, or recognition and the fear of aging and dying. Those fears have often been pushed to the back of our minds and unconsciously put a burden on our happiness.

When we are not aware that we are afraid of something,

it starts invading our brain cells, and we may behave in a manner that impedes our mental and physical well-being. We may project from our fearful mind and create all sorts of unwanted situations, including illness. We eventually become the slaves of fearful minds and the prisoners of fearful bodies that can make us physically and mentally sick at any moment.

Interestingly, we give value to fear because we are under the illusion that it keeps us safe. Indeed, fear can sometimes protect us from danger, as we see in the fight-or-flight response. However, most of the time, we host inner fears that we cumulate from life experiences, and they don't serve any helpful purpose. They only make us feel bad, make our lives unproductive, and poison our relationships. This is why fear is a trap. The first step in overcoming fear is to see it for what it is, something that only exists in the mind, as Carnegie says.

## Anxiety

Our minds are very creative, and they "like to take us into excursions," as my dear friend Jean Houston says.

How we respond to fear is what really matters. There is such a thing as productive fear and even productive anxiety, when we consciously use them to propel us into action. For instance, a student might experience anxiety about failing a test and take the proper steps to engage in studying. Conversely, unproductive anxiety would make the student feel so overwhelmed by the thought of failing that it would interfere with studying and the exam performance.

Fear can be an opportunity for us to go beyond our perceived limits, leading us to exceptional achievements.

We can be triggered to save a life out of the emotion of fear and jump into the ocean to rescue someone who is drowning. However, in many instances, we become paralyzed rather than proactive in the face of fear, because our mind is not processing it in an efficient, positive way.

Fear is not just an emotion that we experience in specific situations. We all have fears that sit in the back of our minds, whether it is not getting what we need, or losing what we have, or not being loved or appreciated. We may fear old age, illness, and death itself. We may worry that something might happen to us or our dear ones, and we might project ourselves into an imaginary future that scares us.

"Worrying is using your imagination to create something you don't want," says Abraham Hicks.

Worrying is counterproductive, negative thinking that exhausts our energy and acts as a blow to the mind, leaving us with poor thinking and discernment, often resulting in actions that don't serve us. Being *concerned* about something or someone is a normal, caring reaction. It can help us find solutions to the problems we face in our lives. However, when it starts causing worry in our minds, it becomes unproductive and harmful. So we have to be aware of what we are doing with the smallest concerns we have in our lives. Oftentimes, we turn them into unnecessary turmoil, and they distract us from the thought that we should be grateful to be alive in the first place.

The key is to identify which fears are healthy and stimulating and which ones lead to destructive anxiety and worry. Identifying them as soon as they appear to us, or even before they arise, is the way to gain control over anxiety.

## Trauma

We are exploring more and more the effects of psychological trauma on the body and how it creates an impact at the cellular level. This would explain how deeply traumatic experiences, such as physical abuse, have the potential not only to trigger major illnesses but also to imprint some information in the genes that could even be carried on to the next generation.

When the mind is oppressed for years with conscious or subconscious negative emotions, it puts a burden on the body that often translates into a chronic disease. There is a cascade of physiological events that take place when the body is under stress that affects our hormones, starting with cortisol. When stressors are small and short-lived, the body rebalances itself spontaneously, calling on its innate ability to bring back homeostasis. However, when the mind is constantly in a fight-or-flight mode, it causes a constant imbalance in the body, where health cannot be sustained.

Interestingly, the most harmful thoughts are often those we are not aware of in our background mind chatter. They are so deeply imprinted in our psyche that we don't even know they are present anymore. They become very insidious and tend to condition every thought we have and every decision we make. They come from the trauma we have experienced in this life or have inherited from our family lineage and ancestry.

Any fearful experience creates trauma, as we all process and interpret fear from our own personalities, upbringing, and conditioning. In other words, you don't need to be the victim of a violent attack to become traumatized, and we all carry our own set of trauma scars. The most obvious reaction to trauma is the need to protect ourselves from perceived danger. It gets in the way of experiencing much joy in life. It's especially true in human relationships. We are the happiest when we exchange love with other people, but we restrict ourselves because are afraid of being hurt. This is where we most experience the illusion that fear keeps us safe, while it actually deprives us of the meaningful and beneficial parts of life.

Bringing traumatic thoughts into consciousness takes a great commitment, as it can be a long, painful journey, most often undergone with a psychotherapist or a life coach. Although this is an essential step, the tools that help us reach our health threshold can greatly accelerate the clearing of trauma. We need to actively flush the traces of past events out of our subconscious mind, and the body needs to be involved in this process.

Also, we cannot readily explain every emotion we have, especially fear. There is not always an objective reason to be afraid; phobias are perfect examples of that. They can be so debilitating that some people cannot even leave their homes anymore. In those extreme cases, which are not rare, the mind acts as a terrorist over the body, keeping it from enjoying life.

What we need to know is that the body has an innate intelligence that can rescue us when we call on it. We just have to take the steps to maintain the health threshold to find trust in life again. Sometimes fear just catches us so we can bounce back with more strength. I have seen this in many patients who experience panic attacks. Going to the extremes of fear can teach us so much about who we are.

When patients tell me they have panic attacks, I know that they are going through an important phase of their life, where major changes can occur. Panic attacks shake them out of their daily reality in ways they can't ignore; therefore, they can be a calling to transformation and empowerment. I, myself, know about anxiety, phobia, trauma, and panic attacks, and I want to share with you how I learned to overcome them to find deep joy and immense appreciation for life.

## Panic Attacks

Those who have experienced panic attacks know the overwhelming sensation of a pounding heart, the shortness of breath, and the overall feeling of total helplessness.

Like Melanie, the patient I spoke about in chapter 2, I had horrendous panic attacks as a young mother. I was equally afraid of taking any antianxiety medication, so I tried controlling them on my own.

Rather than fighting fear or fearing fear itself, I created an intimate relationship with it. When a panic attack would strike, I would lie down and use the intensity of fear to reverse the process. This is how I discovered that a fear was a high-energy state that could be transformed into a healing tool.

Having spent many years in Florida, I compare panic attacks to a hurricane. The winds are blowing so strongly that everything is shaking out of control. During these episodes, it is the high energy of fear that is blowing throughout the body. When we capture this intense energy and funnel it down into a point of focus, we stop the chaos. I intuitively found relief by bringing the focus to my chest and into the heart.

Years later, when I became familiar with the work of

the Heart Math Institute and a heart-opening spiritual practice, which we will discuss later, I understood why it was so helpful. Eventually, my whole body and mind would calm down, and the panic attack would be over. The attacks became shorter, and I found more depth in the relaxation and built more strength afterward. When they came back, I would think, *Oh, just another one of those,* and I was less and less afraid of them. At a certain point, I had built such resilience that when I sensed the feeling of fear wanting to arise, I was able to completely shut it down. What I understood through these dreadful moments is that we have the power within us to transcend fear by transforming it into healing energy. The concept that fear could transform into a healing force came to me during the 2020 pandemic. When so many were experiencing fear at the same time, could we use it to serve a collective healing purpose?

From my standpoint as a physician, I want to prevent panic attacks from occurring in the first place. Like any other symptom, these attacks are a disruption of our physical and mental balance. The more we maintain the health threshold, the more we develop core strength and the less vulnerable we are to fear. It just won't get into our system anymore.

"Illness can kill the body, but depression can kill the spirit, and we have been more skilled at finding cures for physical diseases than we have for depression."

# Chapter 9

# Depression versus Oppression

Illness can kill the body, but depression kills the spirit.

Depression has become such a common diagnosis that we see younger and younger people taking antidepressants, which don't necessarily work and have a whole range of side effects. There are ways to regenerate and sustain a state of joy that is not dependent on the events and the people in our lives—and certainly not on a pill .. or two or three, as we see an escalation in the prescription of psychiatric medications that is so hard to discontinue.

Depression is a state of stagnation. In depression, things function at a depressed level, a slower pace, a lower intensity. The mind is either oppressed by invasive negative thoughts or it has exceeded its ability to create new or productive thoughts. This lack of thought creativity can translate into being stuck in a hopeless cycle and giving up.

We may be crawling under the burden of mental toxins and feel oppressed by the weight of our thoughts. Any negative thought, whether it comes from fear from the past, anxiety about the future, burnout, or a bad habit of making negative judgments, acts as a mind toxin.

We can get stuck looking at an uncertain future for ourselves, our children, our planet, and even our galaxy! While those concerns may be valid, we have to avoid getting overly anxious and depressed.

Sometimes fear of the unknown can make us more proactive, and we channel the stress into healthy action; in many cases, however, it freezes us, and we keep ruminating on potential negative scenarios. All that mind chatter—the mind that scares itself through its power of imagination—is what we need to gain control over. In our stressful society, it takes more effort to sustain positive thoughts than negatives ones, and those toxic invaders can easily take over. Eventually, burnout, often characterized by depression, overwhelms the mind, and it cannot lift itself up anymore from the weight of all these thoughts.

When we burn out, the brain, which is supposed to act as a sophisticated center for daily operations, future planning, and creativity, becomes a ghost town where nothing is happening. It is as if there has been a power outage—and there was indeed, because we were cut off from our inner source of light.

We cannot take depression lightly, and as a matter of fact, my main goal is to take patients out of depression as soon as possible and prevent it from happening to anyone. Slow brain waves come from low vibrations. Every time we function at a lower frequency, we lose an opportunity for our brain and for ourselves to thrive, and we move backward.

The spirit is the force that propels us into life and carries us through. It is always with us, wanting to break through and express itself. We cannot kill the spirit, but depression can oppress it so much that it is silenced. Deprived from the vital expression of our spirit, we can't accomplish very much or enjoy anything. We can recall the spirit through meditation, and it will surely be there to rescue us.

## Physically Induced Depression

Depression can originate in the mind, but it can also be initiated by physical imbalance. When we are under stress over a long period of time, our hormones and neurotransmitters get out of balance, our nutrients are not absorbed well, and our ability to generate energy decreases. As a consequence, we start feeling tired, anxious, and overwhelmed by tasks that we once easily performed. We lose our motivation and ability to enjoy life. This happens because we fall out of the health threshold, and we are not in a state of vitality anymore. It is important to catch and address depression in its early stages because it can further threaten our health, just as it does every time we don't function at the health threshold. When it comes from physical causes, depression can be easily resolved even without medication by recreating the physical equilibrium. Sometimes I see patients who have exhausted their nutrient reserves by over-exercising, and all it takes is replenishing them and giving the body some rest. More frequently, declining levels of estrogen and testosterone can trigger symptoms of depression. As soon as we start hormone replacement, patients feel reenergized and happier.

Antidepressants are not always the answer, and doctors need to find out what the cause is before prescribing them because they might not work, and they might have significant side effects. Moreover, some people have genetic mutations that alter the metabolism of these drugs, and they might actually feel worse on them.

While medications are indicated for severe depression, breathwork, meditation, and practicing positive thinking have proven to be very helpful in cases of mild depressive symptoms. When we reinforce positive thoughts, the mind naturally turns away from negativity. At first, it takes conscious effort to focus on hopeful and happy thoughts when we are depressed, but the key is to just practice it and observe how over time the mind shifts. Optimistic thoughts and a positive attitude create magic in our lives. Optimism is creating a momentum toward happiness, which motivates us to embrace new journeys and connect with new people, and it takes fear away. There are studies showing that we can change our brains with our thoughts. The more positively we think, the more positive thoughts we have. This in turn creates new behaviors that can be life changing.

Recognizing that we are not the same person we were a moment ago shows us that we have no reason to hold on to the old person we were if we don't want to. This gives the mind the power to transform itself. When we hold on to the past, we freeze the momentum to evolve that we were born with. We are designed to move forward and create, and as soon as we stop this movement, we stagnate and don't create anymore.

Fearlessness stems from being able to generate forward movement at any moment in our lives. This is why I focus on taking depressed patients out of the stagnation that thought rumination creates. Rather than sitting with their thoughts, going deeper into their feelings, and analyzing the reasons why they are sad or angry, I ask them to see what happens when they stand up, go out, and meet the world. It may seem at first that everything out there is dull and unappealing, but eventually, they will see, hear, touch, smell, or taste something that will ignite a spark of hope in their hearts. This is how they reconnect with the universe and its forward motion and get back on the ride of life.

We are like electrical generators, in the sense that we can create inner light. Most of us experience some form of stagnation or depression at some point in our lives. Our existences are not a linear line from beginning to end and can feel like a roller coaster for some. We have joy and sadness; this is all part of life, and we are here to learn from our emotions and master them. Viewing our vulnerability as a human trait that serves us instead of judging it as a weakness helps us overcome suffering, and the light that comes through as a result is extremely empowering.

"The secret of change is to focus all of your energy, not on fighting the old, but on building the new."

– Socrates

# Chapter 10

# Understanding Addiction

One of the by-products of a highly stressed modern world and a lack of healthy balance is addiction.

As we try to find ways to calm down the body and the mind, our natural tendency to want more of the things that feel good to us can become an issue. The brain loves the surge of dopamine that satisfies a craving. Whether it's sugar, coffee, shopping, gambling, exercise, work, excitement, drugs, or alcohol, we all have a high potential for addiction. Some are more harmful than others, but they all can hurt us down the road. A sugar addiction can lead to diabetes, over-exercising can cause dehydration and hormonal issues, and gambling can ruin us financially. All these are the result of something we have used in excess that has thrown us out of balance.

When we are stressed or depressed and dopamine levels are low, it is easier to fall into addictions. We may start taking substances that alter our moods, such as antianxiety drugs, street drugs, and alcohol, and we may become addicted much faster.

What those drugs are really doing is forcefully altering our inner pharmacy, making us their slaves. The drugs trigger the release of neurotransmitters that we can actually generate ourselves naturally with a combination of steps to reach our health threshold.

## Alcohol and Drugs

"Being human is a condition that requires a little anesthesia." This quote from the movie *Bohemian Rhapsody* caught my attention because I do believe that we need a break from our minds sometimes. There is nothing wrong with acknowledging it, but of course the last thing we want is to use harmful substances.

Drug and alcohol addictions have become so prevalent, and it is very difficult to break free from them. We need to go much deeper into the reasons why people get addicted in the first place. Addictions are often initiated by a life situation—a loss, a divorce, or financial struggle, for example—that triggered depression and the need to self-medicate to get ahead.

However, there could be more deeply ingrained reasons that predispose people to addictions.

Very sadly, I have heard patients telling me that they felt they didn't belong anywhere and were misunderstood, or that no matter what they were doing, they were not good enough.

Thinking that we are too different or less important than other people is the first mistake we make when considering our existence. We are all in this world together, and each of us is a significant piece contributing to the big puzzle of life. We can't minimize the importance of the role each of us plays on this planet; when we do, we get in the way of universal organization.

Our stories may sound different, but they are not; they all involve wounds, disappointments, and beautiful moments of joy and peace. Our existences are both powerful and fragile. At times, we are heroes, and at other times we are defeated. In those moments when we are not at the top of our game, we need to have efficient tools that bring us back up as fast as possible so we don't fall into a cycle of stress and depression.

## Pain Medications

Sometimes addictions occur as the result of pain management. Addiction to pain medication is unfortunately still too frequent. Doctors need to help their patients out of pain, but unfortunately, they don't have anything else to aid them other than those drugs. Maintaining the health threshold can tremendously help with addictions.

First, let me tell you what happened to very dear friend of mine, Lisou. She is a powerhouse and a perfect example of how the mind can rule over the body. Her positive outlook on life gives her such mental strength that she makes lemonade out of lemons in the worst situations.

She was in her mid-seventies when she fell on her back and broke a vertebra. It turned out to be a small fissure that they were able to fix with a minor outpatient procedure by injecting some bone cement.

She came from France to stay with me so I could help her recover from the minor spinal procedure. The orthopedic surgeon had put her on opioid painkillers after the surgery, as is usually done, but it had been three months, and she was still taking them regularly.

When she arrived, I was shocked by how weak the procedure had left her and the level of pain she was still experiencing.

She was also confused about why she didn't feel better when the procedure had taken care of the small fracture, and why she had to take the pain medications that were making her so tired around the clock. Yet, every time she delayed taking the pills, she was in pain again.

She was aware that the medication had caused a cycle that was hard to break. The fear of being in pain was bringing her focus to the injury site and somehow reactivating the pain.

She needed to start moving again to detour her attention from the injury site, so I decided to take her to the gym and become her personal trainer! At first, she couldn't even lift her arms up from her waist, but with patience and determination, her strength came back.

My plan was to help her taper down the medication very gradually, but she did it on her own much faster and was completely off in two weeks. I gave her a strong supplement regimen to help with bone loss and improve her muscle mass and metabolism.

We worked with powerful breathing techniques to enhance her energy levels and improve her upright posture to give more support to the back. I also taught her how to mentally get in her body and observe it from inside to continue the healing process. We created a special mental visualization exercise, a mind-guided body scan to help her discover her inner doctor.

"I follow the healing power
in my body to manifest
perfect health."

— Louise Hay

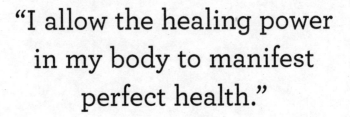

"I allow the healing power
in my body to manifest
perfect health."

- Louise Hay

# Chapter 11

# Regaining Power over Your Health

"Health is freedom from disease and pain, the condition of being sound in body, mind, or spirit." This is the definition of *health* according to *Merriam-Webster Dictionary*.

This is also how I define the health threshold, an unshakable balance in body, mind, and emotions. "Spirit" is an abstract concept open to interpretation, and I prefer using the word "emotions" which emanate from the heart, our inner spiritual center. At the health threshold, we can regenerate health as energy circulates freely throughout the body and the mind.

We can find this fine-tuned equilibrium within ourselves, a frequency at which we preserve our health. We just have to learn how to maintain this balance as if we were using a tuning fork.

So what would it mean to regain power over your health?

It starts by knowing that in our changing health care situation, you are in charge! You are the most important member of your medical team who can participate in creating this equilibrium. You can find your self-healing potential by learning how to use your inner resources to rebalance your health.

## Conscious Health

Eating and sleeping well, exercising, and avoiding toxins is what we commonly understand when we talk about being health conscious. This means that we understand that health is important, and we are taking the right steps to nurture it. However, having full consciousness about our state of health goes way beyond these measures.

I support and recommend healthy lifestyle habits as part of the health threshold program, as I believe they are a baseline to maintain health. Health consciousness goes further and deeper. It involves the awareness of how we feel and how we think. We believe we are fairly in touch with ourselves until we start to practice paying close attention to our bodies and becoming more tuned to what is happening to it.

When we are fully present in our body, we intuitively know when we are in a state of homeostasis (balance). We can sense the slightest deviation from our health threshold, and the body will give us feedback on where the disruption is occurring. This a fine observation of what is going on inside ourselves. This whole universe of cells and chemical reactions within us that we spoke about in the previous chapters is expecting your mindful visits to collaborate with you at all times.

We don't want to wait until our body calls our attention with pain or malfunction. We need to be in touch with it so we can see the early warning signs and shift them. In medical practice, we use x-rays and body scans; at home, we use mind-guided body scans.

Health consciousness is a collaborative process with your doctor. What you report from your insight are the subtle symptoms that the doctor can target to help you optimize your health.

This is the *diagnosis evaluation* part of physical consciousness. The other part is the *healing phase*, when you act as your inner doctor. This is when you can activate your inner pharmacy to rebalance your health. Your doctor can support you by prescribing medications or supplements, but you are empowered to enhance their effects, so you only need to ingest the smallest dose possible.

As for everything, where your attention goes, energy flows. So when your attention is directed to this amazing body that was given to you to host your precious mind, and when you are in full appreciation of this gift, you start becoming more conscious of how much you need to honor it. Most of the time, we take for granted this incredible factory that functions twenty-four seven to keep our hearts beating so we can have this life experience!

## Cellular Regeneration

Reaching the very fine balance of the health threshold is the key to health and longevity. We regenerate physical and mental health from inside our cells, and this is how we achieve lasting, vibrant health.

There is a concept in Ayurvedic medicine that the body is not just a vehicle, it is the projected image of who we are in spirit.

According to medicine, the body is the projected expression of our DNA. According to psychology, the mind is the projection of past experiences and conditioning.

In brief, we are quite complex creatures, and we have to deal with it all—the body, the mind, and the emotions.

Before this new era of collaboration with holistic healers, addressing any component of life other than the body was not expected in medical practice. People don't usually go see a physician to be prescribed yoga, and I used to have a hard time convincing my patients to start a meditation practice to calm their minds. Thankfully, things have changed so much that, upon the request of my patients, I have included some powerful healing breathing and meditation techniques in my treatment plans.

Over the past few years, I went a step further using breathing and meditation. Inspired by Jean Houston's extraordinary teachings on the quantum field, I have started teaching patients how to take mental trips through their bodies to heal themselves.

The breathwork, the meditation, and the mind-guided body scans are all part of the antiaging and regenerative process that completes the physical support from functional medicine to bring us to our health threshold. Among many benefits, including elongating telomeres, yoga and meditation increase BDNF (brain-derived neurotrophic factors), which is known to improve brain function. In times where our brains need to function better and faster every day and where dementia is on the rise, this is certainly worth our attention.

Learning how to regenerate the cells in our bodies requires our conscious input and a commitment to our health. We put so much effort into our work and our relationships, but why do we neglect our health, the thing we need the most to survive and thrive? Our natural tendency is to take health for granted until things break down.

It is the regenerative process that keeps us alive and also changes us. We are not the same person we were last month or even a second ago. Our cells are changing our physical bodies as we speak, but our thoughts are changing too. We don't have the exact same thought twice; it's usually expressed in another way or colored by a slightly different emotion.

Our bodies, our thoughts, and our emotions make us who we are, and we cannot have the same cell composition in our bodies, the same thoughts, and the same emotions at two different given times. This pattern of change is what offers us the flexibility to evolve.

"Knowing thyself is the
beginning of all wisdom."

- Aristotle

# Chapter 12

# Know Thyself

Knowing who we are is very empowering.

We want to understand our own thinking and reactions to the events of our lives and our relationships to keep healthy minds.

It is equally important to learn how our bodies work to have vibrant and lasting physical health.

Let's delve further into our miracle factory with a simple overview of some of the systems that maintain life and regulate our physical bodies.

As you read through these descriptions and visualize the processes, you will develop a better sense and deeper awareness of what is happening inside of you.

The understanding and appreciation of these miraculous activities that take place in our bodies is an empowering step toward our health threshold.

Going through these systems is preparation for the mind-guided body scans.

## The Respiratory System

Let's start with the place where life starts. We took our first breath of life upon exiting the womb, and we will keep breathing to stay alive until we leave the earth.

We inhale air charged with oxygen through our nose and

mouth. It goes down into a tube called the trachea, which separates into two branches called bronchi, one going to the right lung and another one to the left lung. Those bronchi, in turn, separate into multiple branches called bronchioles that distribute to the whole lung. At the end of each of the thirty thousand tiny bronchioles in each lung are little sacs called alveoli, with lots of small blood vessels. It is in the alveoli that oxygen exchange occurs.

What does this mean?

When air goes down into the lungs, it carries the oxygen molecules that we inhale. When the air reaches the alveoli, our red blood cells pick up the oxygen molecules and carry them from the lungs into the heart, and then the heart sends it to the whole body.

The blood that goes into the lungs is deoxygenated, meaning that the red blood cells don't carry any oxygen and are on their way to load it up in the alveoli. The blood that exits the lungs is oxygenated, and as a result, the red blood cells turn more reddish. This is how we distinguish veins from arteries; veins are bluish because they carry deoxygenated blood, and arteries are red because they carry oxygenated blood.

The heart plays a central role in circulating oxygen in the body. It pumps the blood into the lungs so it can get its oxygen, and then sends the oxygenated blood throughout the body, up to the brain, down to the digestive system, the reproductive system, our legs and arms.

Without oxygen, our organs can't survive, and the heart generously and actively gives nourishment to the whole body, like a caring mother. There is much to be said about the heart both as a physical organ and a place of spiritual reference.

## The Digestive System

The digestive system consists of the mouth, throat (larynx), esophagus, stomach, liver, gallbladder, pancreas, small intestine (small bowel), and large intestine (colon). Each contributes to a step in the digestive process that allows us to utilize the foods we eat for growth and energy. They all play an essential role, and the process is so precisely orchestrated that when one step is impaired, we can suffer from health issues.

The food is carried down the gastrointestinal tract by movements initiated by our parasympathetic nervous system (which we will address later), called peristalsis.

Digestion starts as soon as we put food in our mouth. The enzymes in our saliva soften the food to make it easier to swallow with the throat. It then goes down through the esophagus and into the stomach, where it is further dissolved by stomach acids and enzymes. The stomach is an acidic environment by design, as it is meant to break down food aggressively. It mixes and grinds it to make it the consistency of a liquid paste.

As the semidigested food passes slowly into the approximately twenty-foot-long small intestine, the pancreas pours in more enzymes, and the bile from the gallbladder is released to break down the fats. In the small intestine, nutrients are retained to be absorbed into the bloodstream; the rest of the food keeps moving along and into the large intestine.

The liver acts as a detox center that purifies the nutrients that circulate into the bloodstream.

It eventually arrives in the approximately five-foot-long large intestine in a liquid form, where the water content is removed to leave only the waste material and bacteria. These bacteria, however, play a crucial role, as they stay there to produce important vitamins. Whatever is left gets expelled into the stools.

This is what happens every time we put a piece of food in our mouth, and there is much more to it when we go into the chemistry and cellular aspects of the process. There can be many consequences when any part of the digestive system does not function optimally, and stress can be a major insult to our gut.

## The Nervous System

The nervous system is made of our brain and spinal cord, to say the least. We also have a gastrointestinal (enteric) nervous system, which is very sensitive to stress, hence the reason we see so many GI complaints in medical practice, starting in childhood.

For the purpose of this chapter, let's look closer at the somatic and autonomic nervous system that rules our brain and spinal cord center. The somatic part controls body movements, which we voluntarily initiate in our brain. Let's say you think about reaching out to pick up your phone on the table; your arm extends, and your hand grabs it. The somatic branch is what becomes most noticeably impaired when there is brain injury, because the person may have trouble moving or walking.

The autonomic nervous system may sound more complex because it involves involuntary movements. It means we don't have direct control over them. However, we may learn how to control some of them indirectly. For instance, we can tell our heart to beat slower, just as we can tell our hand to pick up the phone, but we can engage in a breathing exercise that will bring the heart rate down.

The autonomic nervous system is made of two parts, which you may be most familiar with—the sympathetic and the parasympathetic branch. Overall, the parasympathetic activity is calming to the body and mind, and the sympathetic one is exciting to them. For instance, the peristalsis that moves the food down the digestive system is ruled by parasympathetic action. The more relaxed we are, the better we digest. When we are stressed, in a fight-or-flight mode, we are in sympathetic mode, which inhibits peristalsis. This is one of the reasons we can have a bellyache when we eat under stress. The autonomic nervous system also sends signals to our glands where our hormones are produced. Any dysregulation triggering too much sympathetic or parasympathetic activity can lead to hormonal imbalance.

## The Endocrine System

Our endocrine system generally releases optimal amounts of hormones until the age of thirty-five, after which it starts gradually declining.

The pituitary gland is the main director of the endocrine system, as it sends orders to other glands, the thyroid, the adrenals, and the ovaries and testes so they can produce hormones.

The two other glands that produce hormones are the pineal gland and the pancreas. The pineal gland independently produces melatonin, which is important for sleep. The pancreas is an organ that is also considered a gland because it produces insulin, which lowers blood sugars.

The pituitary orders the release of two vital hormones: thyroid and cortisol. It sends a signal to the thyroid gland to produce the T4 thyroid hormone, which is converted to T3 into the blood. T3 is the active form of thyroid hormone that controls our metabolism and many other functions in the body.

It also orders the adrenal glands to release cortisol, the stress hormone, which primarily keeps us alive by maintaining our blood pressure. Without any cortisol, we would die within a few days!

It also directs female ovaries and male testes to produce sex hormones: estrogens and progesterone and testosterone. Female health is more complex, as it involves two hormones, estrogen and progesterone, which both play important roles, whereas men produce only testosterone in their sex organs. In addition, estrogens break down into three different forms, which need to be monitored in estrogen therapy.

How things are organized at the level of the pituitary is quite interesting because each hormone affects the other and sends a message back to the pituitary to produce more or less of them. So, when we lack a hormone, it may also decrease another one, and when we supplement with hormones, we need to be aware that it may affect other hormones. In functional medicine, we talk about the hormonal symphony, where all hormones are in balance, contributing to optimal health.

Part of my specialty as a functional medicine doctor is hormone supplementation, which I studied extensively during my fellowship. When it comes to prescribing hormones, it is essential to be knowledgeable about the endocrine system and its processes, as hormones have a much stronger and direct impact on us than nutrients (although nutrients should also be recommended with caution, as we will see).

## The Immune System

In the scope of preventing illness, this is undoubtedly the most critical system we need to preserve.

The immune system acts as a barrier to invaders, such as viruses and bacteria. It prevents us from getting ill but also helps us fight illness once it is here. When it is well balanced, it controls the occurrence of autoimmune diseases and even the growth of cancer cells.

However, our immune system is very vulnerable to the effects of stress, and when it is altered, our body is like a factory without any supervision.

It can become too weak to prevent and help fight illness, or it can become too active and turn against the body.

The "cytokine storm" seen in the advanced stages of coronavirus infection is an overwhelming response of a dysregulated immune system.

The immune cells in our body receive signals that tell them what to do.

What happens in our body when we get sick is mind-blowing. It may even sound like a cartoon when we described it, and it's hard to imagine that we are actually hosting this process!

I often give an overview of the immune system to my patients when they ask me why they don't need an antibiotic to help heal a cold.

We have a powerful army of white blood cells that are here to do the job of attacking microbes or any foreign invader that dares to enter the body. Those cells have been given descriptive names such as killer cells, helper cells, or macrophages (big eaters). They literally go to war with any organism that gets into the body that they don't recognize. They take the foreign invader away through a very organized intervention, kill it, and swallow it. They even target the GMO particles in gluten and corn that are not meant to be digested and absorbed because they are not real food that the body can use. This results in the many symptoms we see today with gluten intolerance. It's creates a toxic immune reaction.

This incredible defense system, which is here to protect us, can also become a problem when we transplant organs, and we actually need to calm those cells down with strong drugs so they don't cause the body to reject the new organ. Both an overactive and underactive immune system can also cause illness, as those warrior cells may respond too much, causing secondary damages with by-products, or they may not react enough and let the invader win.

When we function at our health threshold, the immune system is naturally in a state of balance, and these white blood cells respond in an efficient and safe way.

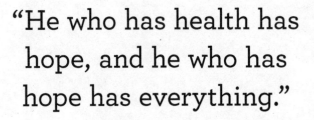

"He who has health has hope, and he who has hope has everything."

– Thomas Carlyle

# Chapter 13

# Breathing for Your Health

I realized the importance of breathing when Dr. Todd, my neurology mentor asked his patients to take a deep breath and a long sigh before starting his consultation. Dr Todd had a saying, that "a sigh has saved many lives." Sighing is a profound and prolonged exhalation that can calm us down instantaneously.

The way we breathe has a significant impact on our nervous system and a regulatory effect on our heart rate and blood pressure. When we breathe deeply, the movement of the diaphragm triggers the Vagus nerve which decreases our heart rate and blood pressure. Stimulating the Vagus nerve causes a parasympathetic response which relaxes us physically and mentally.

In this hectic world, we have become fast, shallow breathers. When we are mentally stressed, we breathe even faster and more superficially, and we only notice it when we are finally able to take a deep breath.

First and foremost, let's remind ourselves that breathing is what brings life to the body. The very first thing doctors do in an emergency setting is secure the airways, meaning taking all measures to make sure that the patient is breathing. Bringing air into our lungs is what keeps us alive and initiates all the other functions in the body.

The way we breathe has a direct effect on our health

because all our organs need oxygen. Fast, superficial breathing is very tiring, whereas slow, deep breathing is energizing. Experienced yogis have learned how to prolong their breath, as they believe that the fewer breaths they take, the longer they live.

Shallow breathing triggers headaches and back pain, but it also causes brain fog and chest pressure that may sometimes feel like a heart attack and prompt patients to go to the emergency room. It can trigger all sorts of digestive issues, like the so-called leaky gut that keeps us from absorbing nutrients. We also have to be aware that, as time goes on, it can lead to a more serious illness.

Deep breathing, on the other hand, expands the chest, contributing to a better posture, which is important especially as we age. It stretches the small intercostal muscles that open up our thorax as we inhale. When those muscles become tight or atrophied, our chest doesn't expand as much, and it becomes harder to take a deep breath.

How often do we breathe to the full capacity of our lungs?

We need to relearn how to breathe in ways that serve us best and use our breath as a powerful healing, disease-preventive, and antiaging tool. Some breathwork can be used to energize and regenerate the body, and some can help calm down the overactive mind. When we are in a calmer, less reactive state, we are also less vulnerable to illness.

## The Effects of Breathing on the Mind

"We can't change our thoughts, but we can change our breathing. Shallow thinking comes from shallow breathing," says Dr. Joseph Michael Levry.

Our level of consciousness correlates to the way we breathe. In order to be in the present moment, we need to be in touch with our breath.

Breathing prepares us for meditation, flushing away our thoughts and relaxing the body. It switches the mind to a positive mode that empowers it to resist outside triggers. The mind is like a muscle that needs to be exercised to become strong enough to establish healthy boundaries.

When we take deep breaths, the brain receives a signal that we are safe and starts shutting down fearful and doubtful thoughts, allowing in peaceful and hopeful thoughts and feelings. There are many variations of how we can breathe deeply, and kundalini yoga practices include countless combinations of breath, sound, and movement. In the appendix, you will find the online access to my breathing programs in which we are using some of these breathing techniques.

As we practice conscious breathing, we also become more present, and in turn, our minds stop going back to thoughts of the past or the future. When we give our full attention to the present moment, we feel more in charge of our lives and our destiny.

Interestingly, the only thing that seems to matter is now, and this is why we are not as afraid that the past or the future may impact us. The moment we are observing takes the whole space, and all our senses are involved in it.

This is why I believe we are so powerful in meditation.

Our senses are enhanced because they are completely focused.

Breathing can also be used to take us out of stagnation. Rhythmic breathing can give new momentum to the mind, and oftentimes after breathwork practice, new ideas come up and we feel energized to act upon them. Breathwork is not only very healing, it is also productive.

Doing breathwork as a group brings the best results. One thing that I always find fascinating is how, as human beings, we connect through the breath. There is something powerful about group breathwork; we all end up breathing at the same rhythm as we become more aware. We have an innate human desire for togetherness that manifests even at the level of the breath.

When my children were afraid and breathing faster, I used to put my hand on their belly and have them inhale and exhale from there along with me. Gradually, their breathing would synchronize with mine, and they would calm down. When we sit by a sleeping baby and listen to their breath, it calms down our own breath.

"The only difference between you and me is that my mind is quieter than yours."

– Dalai Lama

# Chapter 14

# Calming the Mind

Breathing is the bridge between the outside and inside worlds, and it prepares us to calm our minds. Meditation is the focus we need to bring a sense of equanimity and neutrality to our reactive minds. We don't want to shut down our feelings, but we don't want our emotions to take over our lives and become counterproductive.

The practice of meditation helps us calm the body and gain more mind clarity. Consequently, we can better discern which thoughts cause chaos, confusion, and negative feelings and which give rise to joy, peace, and positive feelings.

## Meditation

I interpret the term *meditation* as something that brings us to a fully one-focused, peaceful moment. For some, it is sitting cross-legged and sinking into the void, while for others, it is just being completely immersed in something that captures their mind and takes them away from emotions and thoughts.

In both cases, it helps us calm down the chaos of the thinking mind and provides an opportunity to have a better grasp on our thoughts. Setting aside daily meditative time is important for our health. It is part of maintaining the health threshold because it prevents stress from taking over our health.

It's often said that what we expect is what we create. When we think positive thoughts, we encourage good things to happen, and when we struggle with negative feelings and picture bad outcomes, it usually predicts that things are not going to go well.

## Proactive Surrendering

It may sound counterintuitive, but the best way to become empowered is sometimes to surrender. Surrendering doesn't mean giving up or abandoning our willpower; rather, it means the opposite. It is a mindful decision to decide to create peace within ourselves; it is an action to get into meditation and decide to trust that the world won't collapse when we stop giving it our usual attention for a half hour.

Positive and negative expectations can affect our health one way or the other. They either cooperate in the healing process, or they go against it. We are often told to have no expectations, so we don't get upset if what we wished for doesn't happen. This is a point of surrendering to the laws of the universe. As soon as the mind relaxes, contentment takes place, and we start thinking from a happier place devoid of fear, and this passively creates a state of positive expectations. When we don't expect anything, we intuitively know that whatever happens will be good because it is not linked to the attachment to fear. We are not focused on outcomes, as we know and trust that the universe provides exactly what is needed. Fear is gone.

Fear is an emotion related to time. Fear is in the future, just as grief is in the past. When we are truly present, the mind is focused on the inside, on this place within us that is permanent. Finding that permanent essence is the secret to inner peace. When we find that unshakable core within us, thoughts cannot disturb us.

If we were living every moment with the full awareness of the impermanence of our life, we would be in constant fear. We would be in serious trouble if we became obsessed with the uncertainty of our lives, expecting death to strike at any moment. Uncertainty is unbearable to the human mind, and thankfully, our hearts are equipped with an innate system of trust that saves us in most situations. Instead, we choose to become conscious of the present moment by embracing life without questioning whether or not we will be alive a moment later. This is what we do in meditation, choosing to embrace the present moment and dismissing thoughts from the past and the future.

What we surrender to is the trust that we can let go of control of our lives for a moment, and the world will keep going. Surrendering in meditation brings us to a higher octave and, as a result, a higher state of health. This is an elevated vibration where illness cannot be found, and the more we visit that space, the healthier we become.

When we surrender, we find a state of being that is so powerful it leaves no room for fear. This is the space where our innate wisdom resides, and if we pay close attention, we will get in touch with all the love trying to reach us and heal us, filling us with inner joy and peace. When we reach this place, there is no more sensation of pain.

Being humble and recognizing that our spirit is much more powerful than we are helps us embrace our healing powers. Healing comes from surrendering, not fighting.

## Do Not React

Health is a harmonious equilibrium, and we need to bring the mind and the body to a less reactive state, where the stress cascade won't be initiated.

Some situations can be very triggering to us, and we often feel the need to react to them when we should step back and observe. Ultimately, the key is to learn how to become impermeable to stressors and not to react to them.

We might have to let go of some of the beliefs imprinted in our minds and shift the way we perceive ourselves and the world so we can give ourselves the green light for nonreaction.

However, the more conscious we become of how our reactions affect our minds, our lives, and others, the more we can resist the emotional impulse to respond.

## Don't Take Anything Personally

I will never forget those first words I heard from my ER attending doctor during my first night call. It still helps me in my life every day.

I always wanted to be a doctor, but I had a difficult family situation that kept me from fulfilling my dream in my college years. I went a completely different route and became an entrepreneur. After almost twenty years of running my own business, I decided to go back to school while raising my two children. Medical school was a lot of work, but it was nothing compared to the residency training. I was expecting the long hours and the endless nights, but I never thought it would make me explore my human limits to the core.

I had to be able to react instantaneously to help save a life in the middle of the night and be at full capacity to go on rounds the next morning without any rest at all. When I went home, I needed to be fully alert for my children after that. Needless to say, I was close to fainting or having a nervous breakdown by the end of the first semester in the hospital.

After being the boss of my company for twenty years, what a humbling experience it was to be challenged in this boot camp where chief residents and attending doctors pushed the residents to their edge to make sure they could function under stress and harsh treatment.

I was exhausted and pushing so hard to stay awake when, one night, my chief resident started yelling at me because I was slow. I was fighting so much to adjust to the lack of sleep and overcome my relentless, pounding migraines. This was so unfair! I was about to get back at him when the attending physician took me aside and said, "The most important thing you need to know as a resident is that you shouldn't take anything personally." That very minute, I realized the impact my reaction could have had, delaying the care of a human being to attend a remark that I thought was inappropriate.

It helped me realize how often I had wasted time and neglected important things to make myself right in a situation with another person—and how much grief and stress it had put on me.

Self-love and self-care start by not engaging in the things that are toxic for us. Being offended is definitely not worth a heart attack or even a stomachache. When we take all the steps to be at our health threshold, we don't want anything to compromise that equilibrium. Life already has its sets of challenges that we need to stay strong and balanced for; it is completely foolish to compromise our health for ego pride.

When we don't engage in conflict, the remarks and provocation eventually die down, because we don't give them more power. Meanwhile, we have stayed balanced, happy, and healthy.

## The Word We Say Is the World We See

What we say really matters; our words can have a ripple effect that creates a series of events.

To some extent, the words we say end up becoming our reality because we believe what we say, and what we believe is what we see!

I remember sitting in front of my mirror and practicing Louise Hay's affirmations. At first, it was hard to believe everything I was saying, but I gradually realized the impact of words on my life.

The words that come out of our mouths are infused with our thoughts and feelings. Sometimes our tongue is faster than our minds, and those words that bypass our minds and are spoken spontaneously can have even more power.

We then become the spectator to the movie of a life we didn't want to see unfold in that way.

It is especially true when we speak about ourselves. When we say, "I am capable of doing this," we usually make things happen.

We tend to respect and welcome people who use positive and uplifting words because they make us feel better than those who use negative and pessimistic words. So, why not pay close attention to the way we talk to ourselves and about ourselves?

"When you love yourself,
you become the safest
person to be around."

–Matt Kahn

# Chapter 15

# Love Your Health, and It Will Love You Back

A quote on a grocery bag caught my attention a few years ago: "Treat your body as if it belonged to the person you loved the most." Indeed, taking care of ourselves is an act of self-love.

I always question why we tend to take our health for granted and do things that we know are not good for us.

I met a few centenarians during my nursing home rotations, and the one thing they had in common is that they clearly put their health and happiness first. They may have had many children and responsibilities in their lives, but they didn't let stress run them down.

I remember this 103-year-old lady who was living by herself, cooking healthy foods and keeping a log of her doctor's visits and medications. She also made sure that she knitted or stitched every day, as they were her favorite hobbies. Despite her declining vision, she was keeping up with what was giving her joy rather than complaining about her physical issues. Her positive attitude and dedication to her health were a great inspiration for my antiaging training!

Taking care of our health as a centenarian requires a lot of effort and attention. Most of us can stay healthy by just dedicating a little time to it, getting great rewards.

It starts by paying attention to the way we feel, not going through life with fatigue and pain until we collapse, and getting regulars medical checkups.

Then we need to be protective of our health by adopting a lifestyle that keeps toxins away as much as possible. That involves having a clean diet and exercise, oxygenating the body, and calming the mind.

It also means finding partners in health who can give you the right advice to keep your health in balance.

Finally, loving your health means dedicating some time to restore and regenerate the body and the mind. I always wondered how religions knew that having a day of rest a week, or sometimes more, and fasting were beneficial to people. Our ancestors must have known the power of regeneration and cleansing.

We may not be able to take a full day of rest, in which case meditation can be very helpful. A deep meditation is like a power nap that resets your physical and mental stamina.

## An Extended Meaning of Self-Care

It is often more natural for us to support our loved ones with their health than attending to our own. Yet the most selfless thing we can do is take care of ourselves.

We are taught to nurture our personal health for the sake of our physical comfort, longevity, and having the freedom to enjoy and perform an unlimited range of activities. Taking care of our physical, mental, and spiritual health serves a much higher purpose than we tend to think.

We all know today that the mind and the body are connected and that our thoughts have a very powerful impact on our physical reactions, but there is even more to take into consideration. We contribute to creating a healthier universe for all when we value and nurture our health. Vibrant health at the health threshold holds a positive energy field that works as a positive signal for our destiny.

Whether we agree or not that we create our own reality and that we contribute to the evolution of our universe, we all have acknowledged at some point that our vibration influences the events of our personal lives. When we are in a state of joy, we notice that the people and the events in our lives tend to be in line with our happy mood. We find ourselves in a flow of ease, and our attention naturally detours away from things that cause us distress. There is a lightness in our hearts, and we feel that our vibrating field has been elevated above the struggles and complications of everyday life. When we expand this idea to a broader spectrum, we realize that by elevating our vibration, we contribute to raising the vibration of the universe and all those around us. In other words, when we exhibit positive behaviors, we emit a positive signal that is also healing to others.

It is common for us to talk about a person having good vibes, which means that for some reason we feel good around them. We all emit vibrations that others can perceive through their gut instinct. We may not able to explain this perception through our primary senses, but our intuition is talking to us.

"Music is a higher
Revelation than all Wisdom
and philosophy."

- Ludwig Van Beethoven

# Chapter 16

# Natural Healing Tools

## The Healing Power of Nature / Plants and Animals

Animals are even more sensitive to the vibrations we emit, and some holistic studies show that plants may be too. We live in a world based on communication with other people, animals, and nature. We cannot underestimate how much disconnecting from nature and becoming extensions of wireless systems has affected our physical and mental health over the past decades. We need grounding when we are constantly bombarded by the electromagnetic field, and it's very important to find ways to access nature and recreate the healing power of natural elements in our diet and supplementation.

I will never forget my visit to the temple of Damanhur in northern Italy. It was a mind-blowing experience in many ways, but listening to the music of the plant was one of the most amazing parts of the visit. We went into the forest with a transducer that was conducting the energy of the plants. The transducer was plugged into a plant, and we started hearing a high-pitched sound as if the plant was singing to us. So the first discovery was that plants can emit music as a form of expression and possibly communication. Then the transducer was put in another plant that was emitting a lower pitch, and another one with a different pitch, and more plants, all sounding their energy .. until we had a whole symphony. It was purely magical, and I felt the vibration of this concert throughout my body and my heart.

We then went back into the temple that had been built in the heart of a mountain. We looked at the beautiful paintings on the walls of the cave, retracing the history of humanity since its birth on this planet. Suddenly we were thrown back in time to our ancestral existence when we lived outside the walls of buildings, with clear skies unobstructed by the passing of planes. The guide reminded us how, back then, human beings were directly in touch with the elements of nature, how they lived according to the circadian and seasonal cycles of nature. What I realized is that we had a direct connection to universal forces. In our modern times, we often live remotely from nature, sometimes not even interacting with the trees, the flowers, and the soil. Our food has become synthetic, and we breathe air that is not as pure.

There is a deep, collective desire to reestablish the connection with the goodness of nature, as people are getting more depressed when they are deprived of it. Many adopt pets, and along with the unconditional love they exchange, they reconnect with nature through them.

## The Healing Power of Music

I have had the gift of being around musicians all my life. Born to the beautiful opera singing voice of my father, I now have the joy to witness the musical journeys of my two amazingly talented children. I don't think there has been a day in my life that I have not listened to music, not even during my intense medical residency training.

I always knew music was calming and uplifting but didn't think that it could actually be a very efficient healing tool.

During my night shifts in the hospital, my sleep cycle was completely disrupted, and I couldn't sleep during the daytime, as we were supposed to when we went back home after a thirty-hour night call. Although I couldn't completely fall asleep, I would put my headphones on and listen to meditation music. I would become so relaxed that I felt reenergized after a couple of hours. No matter how much I had on my mind, with all the responsibilities in the hospital and the constant thought that the beeper could go on any minute, I was able to calm down and get my body and mind to rest.

I had listened to a lot of mantra music when I discovered Dr. Joseph Michael Levry's music. It was more than relaxing; it took me into a deep state of inner peace, and I felt more joyful. He explained to the students at the spiritual center Naam Yoga that his mantra music was precisely organized in patterns and rhythms that are meant to heal by rebalancing the body and the mind.

I was very impressed hearing about the medical implications of this particular music.

A study was conducted at the Memorial Sloan Kettering Cancer Center in March 2014 using Dr. Levry's *Healing Beyond Medicine Music* series, and it was published in the *Journal of Pediatric Oncology and Hematology*. The children in the study were treated for neuroblastoma, and they had a significant reduction in pain after listening to the music series, subsequently reducing the need for larger doses of medication during treatment.

Music also conveys a vibration to the body that we can

easily perceive as a strong physical sensation when we are next to a loud music speaker. This same vibration is conveyed at a lower intensity when the music plays lower. So, we don't listen to music only with our ears; we vibrate it throughout our whole body.

Music vibration may also affect us at a cellular level and change chemical reactions in our bodies. Masaru Emoto, a Japanese healer, studied the effects of sound vibration on water and suggested that molecules of water alter their shape under the influence of music. Since our bodies are about 60 percent water, and the cells in our body are surrounded by water, it has to affect their function.

## Finding Your Voice

I also discovered that the sound and vibration our own voices can provide a calming and uplifting feedback to our body and mind.

We should all be encouraged to find our way to singing, or at least get in touch with our voices. I learned this with Roger Love, a brilliant, renown voice teacher who teaches speakers and singers how to gain control over their innate instrument, their voice.

Studying with him has been an amazing experience in discovering the different sounds we can emit and how they can make us feel and impact others.

Most people don't like the sound of their own voice or, like me, don't pay attention to it. I believe that this is a very important part of our body we need to get in touch with.

Finding our voice is an empowering process.

>

"Once you decide that you want to participate fully with mind, body, and soul, the paradigm shift becomes personal. The reality you inhabit will be yours to either embrace or change."

– Deepak Chopra

# Chapter 17

# Into the Heart of Health

## Healing at the Speed of Light

*How I Discovered the Inner Doctor*

I started meditating when I was fifteen, and at that time, I had no idea what I was doing. I had found an old book about yoga that captured all my attention, and I started practicing a few postures as they were shown in the pictures.

I especially loved the shoulder stand posture, where I was upside down with my legs up in the air. It was so relaxing that I would stay there focusing on my toes until I reached a hypnotic state. My mind was clear of thoughts, and I was just floating in a very pleasant space.

A few years later, I explored self-hypnosis through imagery with my dentist. Back then in France, this method was called sophrology, and my dentist was daring enough to use this as a replacement for anesthetics when taking care of cavities. He said that it was working well for "suggestible" people and that there was no need for injecting painkillers. I must have been well prepared by my meditation to become a suggestible patient, because, indeed, I didn't feel anything.

It was so efficient for me that I later gave birth to my first child naturally, just using sophrology. I came to the hospital with my recorded sophrology music and narrative and kept the headphones on throughout the whole delivery.

After a thirteen-hour labor, my ob-gyn came to my room to tell me that he had never seen any woman give birth with a smile on her face. I had given birth in an altered state of consciousness with self-hypnosis, where I could sustain pain without a problem. My pain threshold had become much higher because I was in a state of transcendence.

My meditation practice evolved over the years through many forms of yoga and the teachings of Buddhism.

All along, I have repetitively experienced episodes of self-healing that are still mesmerizing to me.

I used to suffer from terrible hormonal migraines, and I noticed that during my morning meditation, the pain completely vanished. I remember trying to chase the pain or pinpoint it, but in this space and time, it was nowhere to be found. However, as soon as I came out of the meditation, the headache came back.

It is as if there were two different life spaces, one in which I was suffering and another one where I was perfectly fine. Although it was a great incidental discovery to erupt into a state where I could be pain-free, I wished that I could experience it outside my meditation.

Needless to say, it was hard to ignore the drastic difference between feeling so relieved in my meditation and miserable before and after! I had to understand better why this was happening and if other people had this experience.

This made much more sense later on when I started a mentorship with Jean Houston that forever changed my life. Her teachings are derived from quantum science and resonated with my rational mind that couldn't explain those random episodes of self-healing.

I discovered places in the depth of my psyche I had

never explored before and the power that resides within each us.

I learned that our lives are made of multidimensional layers and that they are not separated spaces, as I thought, but they coexist with us. What it meant was that I could extract the pain-free moment, bring into my daily life, and the headaches would go away. All I had to do was become a participant to the pain-free experience rather than a witness.

In meditation, I was just observing; in the state of altered consciousness by self-hypnosis, I was becoming an active player who could integrate the experience. This is the inner doctor I refer to.

It has been fascinating to discover the correlation between these sensorial experiences and the medical findings in conventional and functional medicine. These intuitive healing experiences also resonated with the concepts of Ayurvedic medicine, behavioral and sacred psychology, and quantum theories; it was all coming together. We have the potential to self-heal and create lasting shifts in our health.

Considering how my spiritual teachers conserve their health and keep their youthfulness, this spiritual conversation about health has to take place.

I am grateful for the healing journey that had brought me to a resilient state of health and vitality. All this self-exploration and discovery has been mind-blowing and wonderful, but what makes me really happy is to now to be able to share it and help other people find their inner doctor.

## The Field of Energies

As we become more receptive to the concept of energy that Eastern medicine has been using for thousands of years, we see a new field of integrative science growing. This body of holistic research is providing new answers where Western science was reaching a plateau.

Have you ever given some thought to how x-rays, ultrasound, and magnetic frequencies (MRI) can go through our skin cover and look inside our bodies without having to open them up? They are all based on energies, vibrations, and frequencies that are gathered from the world we live in and put together to materialize into images that our eyes can see. We are bathing in those energies, and as we have explored them to diagnose what is happening in the body, it's now time to use them as healing tools.

Before we had these incredible modalities, doctors were auscultating patients using their hands and their ears to get feedback from the patient's body. They felt their pulse, listened to their heart, and touched their body to detect the source of pain.

I can't imagine what it was like for a doctor in the 1800s to witness the invention of the stethoscope and x-rays. Suddenly, being able to hear and see inside the body brought medicine to a whole different level.

We have been using these modalities for a couple of centuries, and they have become more and more precise to the point that we can detect the smallest defect (whether it's always a good thing is another debate, as we don't always know if what we see on imaging needs to be treated, but we save lives every day with these sophisticated tools).

All these devices were created using the laws of physics,

whereas blood tests are based on the laws of chemistry. We put those laws into machines and test tubes when Eastern doctors were already using them intuitively.

We also know that energy can be utilized to heal people. Laser therapy, invented in the 1960s, is a perfect illustration of energy healing.

Now, if energy can penetrate us, it's because it is also within us, not only around us. We use a microwave to capture frequency waves, but why wouldn't we be able to capture some frequency waves out there and use them ourselves?

I've had patients tell me that energy healers helped them completely shrink cancer tumors, and I believed them when no other doctor did, even though they had no explanation for how it happened. There was no reason to think that it was all in their heads, as some doctors would say, and even if it was, it worked! The power of the mind and its ability to trust beyond what the eyes can see is huge when we activate it. I was open to trusting that it was possible to heal with energy, and I eventually saw it for myself.

## Light Energy

The light of the sun that regulates the natural cycles we depend on and that produces the heat we need to survive on this planet is also what allows us to see things outside ourselves.

Meditation opens us up to see light inside of us. It happens spontaneously, and it does not come from an external source. Actually, we can be in a completely dark room and see light inside our minds.

Through my meditations, I found that the light that fills

the mind of the meditator can also be carried intentionally to the rest of the body. We can see light filling up our heart, for instance, and that can give us a sense of peace and joy. We can send light to an area of the body that is in pain and start feeling some relief. I sometimes funnel that light down in my mind to a laser beam that targets a certain place in my body, intending to heal it just like a laser device.

I've always wondered how we could enhance medical treatments with light to make them work better. Stem cells, for instance, should logically grow in the body since they grow well outside of it. They don't always though, as something inside of us does not allow it to happen. When we look at treatments that work in vitro (outside the body) and don't work in vivo (inside the body), there may be a chemical reaction blocking it or one that is not occurring to make that happen. In the case of stem cells, we may need to voluntarily and intentionally give them a signal to grow .. and could that be the inner light we see in meditation?

This is the reason I use the visualization of light during the mind-guided body scans. It can be used as a mental healing device.

## Emotional Health

I believe that we could use those energies readily if we were not carried away and confused by our emotions. Just as a laser is completely focused on a beam of energy, our minds could be too, but we are not machines or robots. We have a heart. The world is a big love affair, and if we didn't have love, we would probably be robots.

The Heart Math Institute has been exploring the magnetic field of the heart to prove that its intelligence is superior to that of the brain. In other words, if we could completely think from our hearts, we would be capable of things our minds cannot conceive.

This contradicts the common saying "think with your brain and feel with your heart." I've always thought that heart and brain where figuratively connected, just as they are physically. The heart sends blood to the brain, without which it couldn't survive, and the brain brings back blood to the heart, without which it would have no reason to live.

We may also have limited ourselves to think that machines can perform better than we can because we have not yet learned how to use the potential of our hearts. Our emotions are in fact the teaching tools we need to explore.

When looking at the heart as the organ of life, we may just see a center regulated by electric impulses to pump blood into the body. It's hard to relate this four-chamber organ to a center of emotions. However, when we go into the inner journey of the fantastic voyage, we can see how meaningful the heart's role is in many ways.

The heart gives; that is the generous nature of the heart. It gives life to the body by carrying oxygen to our legs so we can walk, to our arms so we can touch, to our brain so we can think and act, and to all our organs so they can work to keep us alive. It starts with an electrical signal that decided to take place at the time of our conception in our mother's womb and has been going on and on since then. This is the signal that triggers the beating of the heart and the pumping of the blood. What form of miraculous intelligence has sent this electrical signal? This is the mystery of life that we can only observe with profound humility.

I always thought that because we were worth the initiation of such a miraculous process to start with, our existence must be meaningful. We spend time and effort looking for the meaning of our lives outside ourselves when we may be able to find it inside.

Emotions affect our heartbeat and, according to HeartMath, our heart rate variability. So our emotional health is linked to our heart health and the health of all our organs since the heart distributes the blood and oxygen to all of them. When we are calm, the blood flows peacefully at the rhythm it is supposed to have, and when we are agitated or worried, the blood flow becomes scattered, and our organs do not get the same flow of oxygen.

The orthopedic surgeon John Sarno looks at back pain, for instance, as a deprivation of oxygen secondary to negative emotions. This explains why people develop back pain when they are anxious or frustrated. Their backs become more vulnerable, and they injure themselves with the smallest move. If we can injure ourselves due to a negative emotion, then we must be able to heal ourselves with positive emotions.

We often say that love can heal anything. When we are in love, our aches and pains go away. The happiest and healthiest people look at all of life through the eyes of love. They are in love with life, people, animals, and all of nature, but mostly they are in love with their own body, mind, and spirit.

As Matt Kahn says, "When you love yourself, you become the safest person to be around."

"Your genes are coded with information that is enough to recreate the world should you be the only survivor on earth."

– Jean Houston

# Conclusion

In this new era of cross-coaching where we all learn from one another, the time has come to create a united voice for health. The merging of science and spirituality that is taking place all around the world is bringing us to higher levels of health and happiness. There is a reason why yoga and meditation have become so popular. Conventional medicine and psychotherapy don't have all the answers, and we need to call ancient wisdom back into our civilization.

Our modern world is calling us to get out of our habitual life patterns, to function more independently, and to become the best version of ourselves. More than ever, we need to be able to rely on our physical and mental health. We are living in times of transcendence, and we cannot be held behind by a tired, unbalanced body or a burned-out mind; rather, we need to adapt and thrive as we have done for the thousands of years we have been on this planet.

Tapping into the mystical aspect of health is more important now than ever because we need to own all our mystical powers to survive and thrive in this accelerated world. We are the heroes who survived this era, and we need to utilize all the tools we have to be acting as such.

This health revolution is emerging in times when we are contemplating a huge leap in our evolution with the incredible advances in technology and communication. More than ever, we need to get in touch with our human powers so we can collaborate with computers rather than being run by them. We have to step into the mastery of our bodies and minds for the new age to overcome the challenges of our very fast-changing world and become resilient to stress.

We tend to see ourselves as living in a box—a body limited in space and time. This is how we used to think of the earth centuries ago, before we could see that it was part of a greater galaxy system. When we think that we are just randomly going through life in a container that eventually decays and dies after a certain number of years, we are not exploiting the full potential of our lives. This limiting thought itself is the first existential fear we need to overcome in order to get in touch with the powers we host in our bodies and minds.

We may be getting closer to uncovering some of the mystery of human life, and hopefully, this knowledge will enable us to correct genetic errors, stop illness, and control destructive human emotions and behaviors. When we look at the different systems that make life possible, we can see the most advanced level of intelligent organization. Isn't it amazing to think that we are an old species that hasn't changed much throughout thousands of years, yet we have governed this planet and made it a new and different place? Maybe the time has come for us to change as a human species, to adapt to the new planet we have created over the centuries. It does feel to many that we are reaching a time when we need to undergo a metamorphosis to survive, because the virtual computer world we have designed has expanded and accelerated everything. This is what urged me to write this book and share what I have learned and discovered about overcoming the limitations of the human body and mind.

# Appendix

Appendix

# My Philosophy

Vibrant health is a result of Life Force and Balance.
It is a perfect alignment, a fine equilibrium

"The Health Threshold"

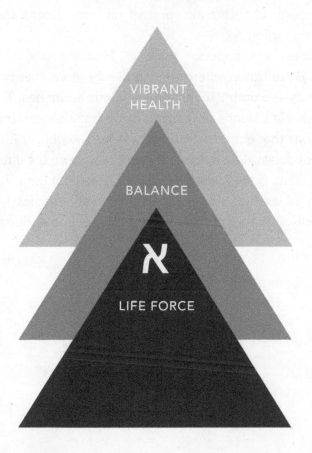

# The Health Threshold

We have a "Health Threshold", a perfect state of equilibrium that creates lasting vibrant health. In medicine, we understand physical balance for the purpose of staying alive. We call this "homeostasis", and it means that we need certain chemical and physical conditions in the body, such as the right fluid balance and a normal body temperature. This homeostasis is of course essential to our survival, but not enough to thrive and protect us from illness and the effects of aging.

There is a superior state of Homeostasis, a fine-tuned equilibrium where we can derive more energy from nutrients and optimize the release of our hormones. This an unshakable balance not only in body, but also in mind and emotions that enhances our natural self-healing abilities to prevent disease. As a result, it also slows down the effects of aging. This is the Health Threshold, a state of high Vitality which is exceptionally energizing both physically and mentally. It makes us feel strong, focused, and enthusiastic.

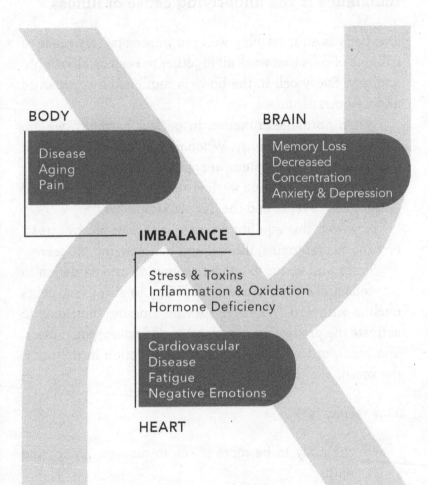

BODY

- Disease
- Aging
- Pain

BRAIN

- Memory Loss
- Decreased Concentration
- Anxiety & Depression

IMBALANCE

- Stress & Toxins
- Inflammation & Oxidation
- Hormone Deficiency

- Cardiovascular Disease
- Fatigue
- Negative Emotions

HEART

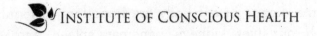

INSTITUTE OF CONSCIOUS HEALTH

# Imbalance is the underlying cause of illness

Our body is an incredibly well programed factory made of trillions of cells that work all together to keep us alive night and day. Every cell in the body is regulated by hormones and neurotransmitters.

When hormones function in perfect harmony, we are healthy and full of energy. When neurotransmitters, which control our nervous system, are released in optimal amounts in our nervous system, we feel uplifted, and we respond better to the events and the people around us.

However, this equilibrium can be threatened by stress, environmental toxins, illness, and by the aging process.

Stress and toxins cause inflammation and oxidation in our cells and our hormones and ability to absorb nutrients decline with age. We need specific amounts nutrients to activate the production of hormones and neurotransmitters. Too much or too little will cause dysfunction in the body, the brain, and the heart.

This results in:

- the body to be more prone to disease, aging, and pain;
- the brain to lose memory and concentration, and trigger anxiety and depression;
- the heart to become fatigued and experience negative emotions that can lead to
- cardiovascular disease.

*All the organs in our body are important in regulating health, our liver, kidneys, pancreas, spleen, and so are our skin, muscles, bones; however, there is a constant interaction between the brain and the heart that influences all the other organs. When the heart beats it sends blood to all the organs and the skin that is charged with the hormones ordered by the brain.

**BODY**

Health
Rejuvenation
Wellbeing

**BRAIN**

Sharp Memory
Focused Mind
Happiness

**VIBRANT HEALTH**

Breathing Therapy
Nutrition & Exercise
Hormone Balance

Cardiovascular
Health
Increased Energy
Positive Emotions

**HEART**

INSTITUTE OF CONSCIOUS HEALTH

This balance in the body, the brain, and the heart corresponds to an equilibrium in Body, Mind, and Emotions which I have called the Health Threshold.

I believe in building a state of resilience that can keep us at our Health Threshold. When we reach perfect homeostasis in mind, body, and emotion, we are less vulnerable to the attacks of toxins, microbes, and the effects of aging.

We also live in a different world from the one our parents and grandparents grew up in. Our soil, our water, and our air have been altered by extensive cultures, pesticides, radiation, and pollution. We are not readily fed what we need by nature as they were. In addition, they were living in a much calmer world with little distraction.

Today, everything around us is evolving and expanding much faster, and we need a strong "seatbelt" to overcome some of the chaotic challenges of these times. Although our human nature is to adapt to new circumstances and create genetic mutations for survival, we now have to learn how to build an extra shielding coat to fight the attacks of environmental toxins, stress, and new viruses. This protective layer needs to be programmed from the inside out and our role in building it is essential.

## Preventing Illness is a Collaborative Task

**We need a balance between conventional and integrative medicine.**

**I believe in both the power of science and of our intuition, and they need to be combined to serve us best.**

Health goes beyond what we can see in lab results and X-rays and we cannot only rely on medical technology. Disease starts before the doctor can see it, and this is when we can stop it without the need for surgical intervention or strong pharmaceuticals that don't always work and create side effects.

Not every illness can be treated as an emergency with medications and surgery. There are certainly instances where only one conventional treatment works, such as an antibiotic for an infection, or a shot of Epinephrine for a life-threatening allergic reaction. However, for chronic issues, or when trying to prevent an illness, we want treatments that can provide lasting results.

I am embracing the shift that is happening in medicine, bringing together the different healing modalities that have already been practiced, sometimes for thousands of years, in different traditions and places. Anti-Aging physicians like me believe in creating one integrated medical world where all options can co-exist. Preventing illness is not just medical intervention, or something patients should figure out at home on their own. It is a collaborative step in health awareness. Prevention belongs to the field of medicine and should be done under the guidance of an educated doctor.

## Epigenetics: Health is something we both inherit and create

We come to this world with a genetic makeup that mostly dictates what we are going to look and feel like. We are the expression of our DNA and the combination of genes we are made of programs our state of health.

However, this health predisposition can be shifted because we can actively change the **expression** of our genes. We can lessen the expression of unfavorable genes by the way we live our lives. This is the new science of Epigenetics which explains how people can turn their health around. DNA reprogramming takes place overtime when we adopt good habits for our health. We are all unique. We have different genes, body and mind types, and life experiences. Therefore, general protocols don't always make sense in medical treatments. For instance, I believe that medicine should be tailored to gender and weight. In the same way, the best nutrition and exercise is the one that fits our unique needs.

## Imbalance in the body is often caused by an imbalance in the mind

Health is **'Multi-Dimensional"**. It is not only a function of the body and its organs. Our thoughts, and especially our emotions, have more involvement in our physical health than we can imagine. We are thinking and feeling beings, and every thought we have creates a feeling that is directly projected on our bodies.

We also have unconscious thoughts that can bring trauma to our minds and insidiously give rise to an illness, sometimes building over many years without us knowing.

As much as the body is an amazing factory that we can understand through medical testing, the mind is an abstract place that is not as easy to interpret and manage. Trying to control it with medications that act on brain chemistry is not the optimal answer.

We have to gain power over our own thinking processes, so we don't become victims of our own thoughts. Good thoughts result in good feelings, and good feelings create good health.

## The way we breathe can change our lives

The one thing that can be of tremendous help to us in controlling our mind is our **breathing**. We go through the day without paying any attention to the way we breathe, when we can actually use it to our utmost benefit.

It's much easier to generate good thoughts when we able to take full deep breaths. The mind has a direct effect on our breathing. When we are mentally stressed, we breathe more superficially, and we deprive our bodies of oxygen. This, in turn, offsets the release and circulation of hormones and neurotransmitters in our system, and over time it can lead to the burn out symptoms of depression.

Breathing has a healthy rhythm just like our lives depend on circadian rhythms. We need regular food and sleep schedules to be healthy. Our hormones and neurotransmitters are produced in a rhythmic manner. We need to re-learn how to breathe in ways that serve us best and use our breath to calm our overactive, overstimulated mind. When we are in a calmer, less reactive state, we are also less vulnerable to illness.

## Redefining Stress

**If I had one prayer, it would be "May we be spared from fear".**

There is "good" stress and "bad" stress. It is not stress itself that directly affects our health; it is how we perceive it and react to it. Stress can actually be stimulating and productive and help us perform at our best. It only becomes toxic when associated with a negative experience in our mind or in our emotional wiring that triggers FEAR.

Fear is the source of many problems in our lives. It affects our mental and physical health, our relationships, and our work performance.

Fear is contagious. We are especially vulnerable to the emotion of fear because our human nature is to doubt and be uncomfortable with uncertainty. While everything around us is evolving at a very fast pace with the incredible advances in online technology and worldwide expanded communication, this feeling of uncertainty for our future is growing.

Moreover, we are asked to be better and stronger than we have ever been in human history and trying to achieve perfection can put enormous amounts of negative stress on us. Working hard doesn't necessarily means we will see the rewards of our labor. We need so much discernment about where to put our efforts that we may exhaust ourselves and have little result. We start fearing that we won't be able to respond to all the demands of our world. The mind automatically goes into worrying about the consequences of not being able to keep up. Our nervous system reaches a saturation point; we may feel overwhelmed, oppressed, or even depressed.

We can lose our health in this endless race unless we start using efficient tools to break out of this stress cycle. Here is where the idea of **balance** can become a life savior. Stressing our system to its utmost potential can propel us to great achievements in life but then, we have to let ourselves regenerate so we can jump even higher if wanted or needed. When we don't take the time to regenerate, our brain becomes saturated by excitatory signals and we experience the emotion of fear.

The brain needs a balance between excitatory and calming neurotransmitters to think clearly. The "brain fog" so many are complaining of comes from overstimulation and lack of relaxation in brain activity.

## Health Consciousness starts with knowing thyself

Our inner world is, for the most part, unknown to us unless we have studied the human body and mind in depth. Even so, we may know where our organs and how they work, but we don't "feel or see" them working.

Through meditation practice, I realized that we can become connected to our bodies and feel what happens every moment. This is very empowering and can help us contribute to our own healing process.

The medicine of the future is a true partnership between the science of medicine practiced by doctors, and the intuitive awareness practiced by patients.

Using guided imagery, *Mind-guided Body Scans* help

us get in touch with our innate healing mechanisms. I believe this is the ultimate collaboration in the healing process.

Up to now, doctors had the objective data from physical exams, X-rays, and laboratory tests, and patients were reporting their subjective experience in the form of symptoms.

Using the self-explorative Mind-guided body scans, patients will be able to better point out the origin of their symptoms, giving their doctors valuable clues. They will also become active participants in the treatment, observing and enhancing the healing process.

# Practical Guide to the Health Threshold

The guide to the Health Threshold is a compilation of advice and tools that address all the layers of health: Body, Mind, and Emotions. Optimizing your health means finding balance in each of these components.

The steps to the Health Threshold provide a framework to start building stress resilience so you can prevent illness and have increased Vitality. This guide will give you tips on how to rebalance and regenerate your body. You will learn about the main hormones and nutrients you need to pay more attention to, the importance of detoxing and reducing inflammation. Beyond a good diet, exercise, regular sleep, and supplementation, you will learn how to optimize these lifestyle interventions and change the expression of your genes to take your health to the next level.

Your body, mind, and emotions are interconnected. Your body can be healthy, but this won't last if the mind isn't. In turn, the mind can be sharp, but it won't last if the spirit is burdened by negative emotions.

You will learn how to have more control over your thoughts and feelings, empower your mind, and build "emotional stamina".

To access to **Health Threshold Guide eBook**
Visit https://evelyne-leone.mykajabi.com

For an introduction to the **Mind-guided Body Scans**
Visit https://evelyne-leone.mykajabi.com

For our Online Health Programs **Love Your Health**
Visit https://evelyne-leone.mykajabi.com

Watch Video: **The Power of Not Reacting** from Dr. Joseph
Michael Levry
https://youtu.be/mhZalV4PRbo

# Recommended Reading

Joe Dispenza, *Breaking the Habit of Being Yourself: How to Lose your Mind and Create a New One.*

Peter J D'Adamo & Catherine Whitney, *Eating Right 4 Your Blood Type – The Individualized Blood Type Diet Solution.*

Steven Gundry, *The Longevity Paradox: How to Die Young at a Ripe Old Age.*

John E Sarno, *Healing Back Pain: The Mind-Body Connection.*

John E Sarno, *The Divided Mind: The Epidemic of Mind-Body Disorders.*

Pamela Smith, *What You Must Know About Women's Hormones.*

Bill Bryson, *The Body: A Guide for Occupants.*

Andrew Newberg & Mark Robert Waldman, *Words can Change Your Brain:12 conversation Strategies to Build Trust, Resolve Conflict, and Increase Intimacy.*

James Maskell, *The Evolution of Medicine: Join the Movement to Solve Chronic Disease and Fall Back in Love with Medicine.*

Jeffrey S Blend, Mark Hyman, *The Disease Delusion: Conquering the Causes of Chronic Illness for a Healthier, Longer, and Happier Life.*

Daniel Amen, *The End of Mental Illness: How Brain Science is Transforming Psychiatry and Helping Prevent or Reverse Mood and Anxiety Disorders, ADHD, Addictions, PTSD, Psychosis, Personality Disorders, and More.*

Daniel Amen, *Change Your Brain, Change Your Life.*

Lissa Rankin, *Mind Over Medicine – Scientific Proof that You Can Heal Yourself.*

Jay Lombard & Dr. Christian Renna, *Balance Your Brain, Balance Your Life: 28 Days to Feeling Better Than You Ever Have.*

Stanley Rosenberg, *Accessing the Power of the Vagus Nerve: Self Help Exercises for Anxiety, Depression, Trauma, and Autism.*

Norman Doidge, *The Brain that Changes Itself: Stories of Personal Triumph from the Frontiers of Brain Science.*

David Perlmutter, *Grain Brain.*

Alberto Villoldo, *Grow a New Body.*

Will Cole, *Ketotarian: The (Mostly) Plant-Based Plan to Burn Fat, Boost Your Energy, Crush Your Cravings, and Calm Inflammation: A Cookbook.*

Mark Hyman, *Food Fix; How to Save Our Health, Our Economy, Our Communities, and Our Planet – One Bite at a Time.*

Andrew Weil, *Healthy Aging: A Lifelong Guide to Your Wellbeing.*

Andrew Weil, *Spontaneous Healing: How to Discover and Enhance Your Body's Natural Ability to Maintain and Heal Itself.*

Amy Myers, *The Autoimmune Solution: Prevent and Reverse the Full Spectrum of Inflammatory Symptoms and Diseases.*

Christiane Northrup, *The Wisdom of Menopause: Creating Physical and Emotional Health During the Change.*

Suzanne Somers. *Ageless: The Naked Truth About Bioidentical Hormone.*

Avrum Bluming & Carol Tavris, *Estrogens Matter: Why Taking Hormones in Menopause can Improve Women's Wellbeing and Lengthen their Lives without Raising the Risk of Breast Cancer.*

Louise Hay, *You Can Heal Your Life.*

Ervin Laszlo, Jean Houston & Larry Dossey, *What is Consciousness: Three Sages Look Behind the Veil.*

Peggy Rubin, *To Be and How to Be: Transforming Life through Sacred Theater.*

Roger Love, *Love Your Voice.*

Thich Nhat Hanh, *The Heart of the Buddha's teaching-Transforming Suffering into Peace, Joy, and Liberation.*

Zelig Pliskin, *Gateway to Happiness.*

Esther Hicks & Jerry Hicks, *The Amazing Power of Deliberate Intent.*

Matt Kahn, *Whatever Arises, Love That: A Love Revolution That Begins with You.*

Brian Swimme and Mary Evelyn Tucker, *Journey of the Universe.*

Jean Houston, *The Search for the Beloved: Journeys in Mythology and Sacred Psychology.*

Jean Houston, *The Possible Human: A Course in Enhancing your Physical, Mental, and Creative Abilities.*

Jean Houston, *A Passion for the Possible: A Guide to Realize Your True Potential.*

Deepak Chopra & Menas Kafatos, *You are the Universe: Discovering your Cosmic Self and Why It Matters.*

Dalai Lama & Howard C Cutler, *A Handbook for Living: The Art of Happiness.*

Doc Lew Childre, Howard Martin and Donna Beech, *The HeartMath Solution: The Institute of HeartMath's Revolutionary Program for Engaging the Power of the Heart's Intelligence.*

Eckart Tolle, *The Power of Now.*

Byron Katie, *Loving What Is.*

David Simon, *Free to Love, Free to Heal.*

Lynne Mc Taggart, *The Intention Experiment.*

Dr. Joseph Michael Levry, *The Divine Doctor: Healing Beyond Medicine.*

Dr. Joseph Michael Levry, *Shakti Naam Yoga: The Gift of Health. Practical Applications of Shakti Naam Yoga.*

Dr. Joseph Michael Levry, *The Ultimate Secrets of Intimacy and Creation.*

Donna Eden, *Energy Medicine: Balancing your Body's Energies for Optimal Health, Joy, and Vitality.*

David Feinstein, *The Promise of Energy Psychology: Revolutionary Tools for Dramatic Personal Change.*

Caroline Myss, *Anatomy of the Spirit: The Seven Stages of power and Healing.*

Caroline Myss, *Why People Don't Heal and How They Can.*

Helen Schucman, *A Course in Miracles.*

Dr. David A. Sinclair, *Lifespan. Why We age and Why We Don't Have To.*

David Simon, *Vital Energy: The Seven Keys to Invigorate Body, Mind, and Soul.*

Dr Deepak Chopra and Dr. David Simon, *Freedom from Addiction.*

Brandon Burchard, *The Motivation Manifesto: 9 Declarations to Claim Your Personal Power.*

Steve Ross, *Happy Yoga: 7 Reasons Why There is Nothing to Worry About.*

Debbie Ford & Wayne W Dyer, *Courage.*

Rudolph E Tanzi & Deepak Chopra, *Super Brain.*

Mike Robbins, *Nothing Changes Until You Do.*

Marianne Williamson, *A Return to Love.*

Louise Hay &David Kessler, *You Can Heal Your Heart.*

Colin Tipping, *Radical Forgiveness.*

Institute of Noetic Sciences, *Behavioral Aspects of Remission.*